COACHING TOP CLU

Pathways to Success

~

John Moore

2001

First Published in 2001 by

Sports Dynamics
15 St. Luke's Place
Cheltenham
Gloucestershire
GL53 7HR
United Kingdom

Tel/Fax: 01242 522638

Sports Dynamics

A catalogue record for this book is available
from the British Library.

ISBN 0 9519543 2 7

Page design, layout and typesetting by Jeff Shambrook.

Printed and bound by Fotodirect Ltd, Brighton, UK.

CONTENTS

Acknowledgements

About the Author

Foreword by Gordon Lord

ACKNOWLEDGEMENTS

Thanks are due to a lot of people who have helped me to complete this book.

To Gordon Lord, David Parsons, Toby Radford, Heather Nash and David Gallagher from the ECB;

to Alan Hill, Derek Mackelworth, John Manuel, and Malcolm Milward from the Staffordshire Cricket Board and the Staffordshire County Cricket Club Youth Charity;

to Tim Heap, Greg Wright, Arthur Pickering, Mary Chapman, Barrie Richards, Alastair Maiden and Nicky Southall for specific contributions and to Duncan Lampitt and the squad of players he led (1998-2000) from Wolverhampton Cricket Club;

to the "Birmingham Post" and the "Sunday Mercury" for permission to reproduce the scorecards in chapter five;

to Simon Collins for his support during the crucial early stages of the project;

to Simon Hollyhead, Geoff Hopkinson and Michael Barraclough for proofreading specific sections and particularly to Neal Gough for proofreading the whole book and making helpful comments;

to Harish Janghra who has shown great expertise in transforming my ideas into diagrams and graphic illustrations;

to my father for his constant support over the 18 months it has taken to write this book.

•

I would like to dedicate this book to my father, to the memory of my mother and to my sister and her family.

John Moore was born in Newcastle-under-Lyme and has played cricket in both North and South Staffordshire. He made Wolverhampton his adopted home in 1968 when he came to teach in the city. He taught in three Wolverhampton schools and, for the last seven years of his teaching career, became headteacher of a large secondary comprehensive school before retiring early to take up a freelance career as a cricket coach.

John played 123 times for Staffordshire in the Minor Counties Championship over a 20 year period and also represented Minor Counties North in the Benson and Hedges Cup competition on 6 occasions.

He has been an active cricket coach since the late 1960's and has kept very much up to date as the coaching scheme transferred from the National Cricket Association to the ECB. He is an ECB Level III coach and Staff Coach III and works closely with the ECB Coach Education department on the Staff Coach tutor training programme. Since the new ECB coaching scheme came into being, he has been a prolific tutor of courses at Level I and II, and has been a major contributor in the design and content of the ECB coaching cards for Level I coaches.

Photograph courtesy of David Peters

He became coach to Wolverhampton Cricket Club in 1998 when they won the inaugural Birmingham and District Premier Cricket League title and followed this by being involved in further success when they won the ECB National Club Championship in 1999.

I have heard it said that John Moore is a 'lucky' coach. If it is true that luck occurs at the intersection of preparation and opportunity, then perhaps what people say is true.

Coaching Top Club Cricket is a 'must read' for any coach who is serious about understanding and developing success. The author's unique blend of experience and skill provide a practitioners perspective on a range of coaching issues relevant to coaches at all levels.

Although there are a number of references to the ECB Coaching Scheme in the book, a thoughtful, open mind and a passion for coaching are the only requirements necessary to enjoy and learn from it.

Be lucky and enjoy the challenge.

Gordon Lord ~ ECB Coach Education Manager

PATHWAYS TO SUCCESS

Wolverhampton Cricket Club won the Inaugural "Birmingham and District Premier Cricket League" in 1998 and the "National Club Championship" at Lord's in 1999. The success coincided with my appointment as coach to Wolverhampton Cricket Club, and led to a suggestion that I write a book explaining what I did.

This book had already been started when it was with great concern to both the club and to me as coach, that in the year 2000 we became involved in a fight for survival to retain our place in the Birmingham and District Premier Cricket League. The second half of the season resulted in what can only be called "The Great Escape!"

This is not a book about technique, or tactics, or physical conditioning, or mental skill development or lifestyle and yet it is about all of them as well. There are other books that deal with each of the above areas in detail and a few will be referred to as sources of further reading.

This book is designed to show how success, and sometimes survival, is believed to be essentially a mixture of preparation, communication and the integration of technique, tactics, physical conditioning, mental skills and lifestyle. While the focus is on success, there is also attention paid to getting the best out of limited resources and suggestions made as to how to deal with events when things are going wrong.

The stressful and, at times, traumatic experience of striving to avoid relegation, especially after two years of outstanding success, hopefully makes the book more plausible with both sides of the coin recognised.

The book can be read from cover to cover, but it can also be entered at any point of interest. For example, if you are interested in "Making Things Happen" in matches, you will be directed towards chapters 2, 3 and 4 along the way for background. On the other hand if you are interested in "The Crucial Factor" of communication, you will be led into seeing how communication dovetails into an overall strategic approach.

The book attempts to:

- *Indicate where you might start*
- *Focus on forward planning*
- *Share practical ideas*
- *Trigger new thinking*
- *Link together the major factors*
- *Give strategies for making things happen*
- *Look at prioritising*
- *Build strong foundations for future development*
- *Promote the ECB coaching scheme*

In the course of writing this book I became increasingly aware that it could grow into something very large and difficult to manage, let alone read. The decision was therefore made to give examples rather than chapter and verse about every aspect that appeared important.

The outcome is frequently more a shopping list of items that it is believed a top club coach should be aware of. The coach can then decide what is appropriate to use, in what circumstance and with whom.

Enjoy the read and "pick and mix" to suit your situation. It's a bit like carrying a rucksack. Only the coach can decide what should and should not go into the rucksack. Some things may be essential straight away while others could be required some way down the line. Other things may be totally inappropriate to your current and/or future needs. That doesn't matter. Take on board what makes sense and throw away that which confuses or complicates matters. Alternatively, put in your rucksack the weight that you can handle now and store some of the other information for a later date. Put it all in the rucksack now and it might become too heavy to be useful.

Whatever route you take, I wish you success as you put it all together. Every coach must take his or her own route because every club needs something different. And in any case, there is always more than one answer to any problem and numerous ways to succeed.

What is advocated in this book cannot guarantee success, but I believe it makes it much more likely.

Be positive, be different. Be you.

Although the title refers to "Coaching", much of what is included is intended to stimulate the thinking of captains and players. The more the players, as well as the coach, understand what goes into making a successful team, the greater chance there is of faster progress in team improvement.

This will not happen overnight. An important dimension of improvement is in determining what the players are capable of handling at a particular time. This concept of player maturity is very important. The culture change could well be very large to start with, but as the building blocks of progress are carefully laid, the foundations will permit more and more ambitious plans.

What a coach might be able to learn from this book and why it is important

Technical and **tactical** aspects have, in the past, dominated the work of a coach, but over the last 20 years, it has become increasingly recognised that team performance is much more than mere technique and tactics. The relative success of other nations, and in particular Australia, has acted as a wake up call to other nations and has led to far reaching changes within the game in England in the late 1990's and early 2000's. It was inevitably only a matter of time for the competitiveness that now exists in the international game to filter into the club game and for every stone to be turned to discover what gives the "winning edge".

A professional approach to a largely amateur game is what this book is all about.

The game has become **physical** in its demands with fielding, for example, light years ahead of even 5 years ago. Physical conditioning is accepted as being very much a controllable aspect of team preparation. The best teams are physically fit for the demands of long spells of bowling or fielding and this fitness supports concentration for extended periods of time when, for example, batting. The modern cricketer who plays at a high standard will increasingly need to be a trained athlete.

Mental toughness alongside many other mental qualities has also been recognised as vital to success. While players bring limitations with them to the game, it is now accepted that many mental attributes can be learned and developed. High class performers in any sport you might care to mention, have acquired and increasingly developed their mental qualities. The link to success is indisputable.

Similarly, it is recognised that diet and nutrition, drink (including alcohol) and dehydration, sleep and other aspects of **lifestyle** have a major effect on a players ability to perform to high standards.

It is the addition of the physical, mental and lifestyle issues alongside technique and tactics that it is hoped connects with the reader in chapter 3.

Chapter 4 also attempts to connect with the reader when it focuses on the importance of **Communication**. Knowledge on its own is of limited value unless it can be accessed by players. The challenge for a coach and captain is one of transmission of information, and of deciding how to engage players actively in the two-way process. Relating communication to individuals, pairs, groups and the team will hopefully stimulate the reader to review their current practice in relation to this 'crucial factor'.

Preparation is big in my style of leadership and chapter 2 is designed to not only offer practical advice, but also, together with chapter 5 "Match Action", influence the reader into reviewing the nature of what they currently do.

Suggestions as to how to use this book

Whatever your level of experience, you will hopefully be challenged by what has been written. For some, it will be the essentially practical and organisational checklists that support the forward planning process as a starting point. For others it will be the philosophical issues that come through asking fundamental questions as to the motives for coaching in the first place.

If you are starting from scratch with a team, it is important to recognise that players are initially more likely to respond if there is practical evidence of planning in the organisation of practice and pre-match routines. The more philosophical aspects involved in the planning of team meetings, shared priorities and targets can be left until later, unless the team are already mature in cricketing terms.

In my first season as coach, I emphasised the **practical** aspects of preparation. This successfully motivated the team and developed the maturity to hold a productive team meeting to plan for the following season, and this maturity has developed substantially with each subsequent season. On the other hand, the 1-1 work with players, concerned with specific aspects of the game, was tailored to fit the maturity level of each individual, and this has also developed substantially season on season.

I am reluctant to tell any coach, captain or player how they should read a book, as each will bring so much that is unique to the process. The guidance below is for the reader for whom it is a preference.

For the coach who is starting out, I recommend the following order:

Chapter 2 – "Preparation" with the 'Team meeting' for reference purposes
Chapter 5 – "Match Action" – the first two examples of successful situations
The technical, tactical and mental aspects of Chapter 3 – "Integration".

The physical and lifestyle issues of chapter 3, the "Communication" issues of chapter 4, the more unsuccessful situation described in example 3 in chapter 5, the more philosophical issues covered in chapter 6 and the concluding chapter 7 can be left until later.

For the coach who is trying to manage a team who are under-performing and who is looking for inspiration I would recommend the following order:

Chapter 5 – "Match Action" – example 3 dealing with an unsuccessful situation.

Chapter 5 – the first two examples dealing with successful situations.
Chapter 2 – "Preparation"
The technical, tactical and mental aspects of Chapter 3 – "Integration"

And the remainder as listed for the coach who is starting up.

For the coach who is already coaching a team and who is seeking to expand their sphere of influence I would recommend the following order:

Chapter 5 – "Match Action" – 'Making Things Happen'
Chapter 6 – "The Coach" – 'Rising to the Challenge'
Chapter 2 – "Preparation" – 'The Heart of Success'
Chapter 4 – "Communication" – 'The Crucial Factor'
Chapter 3 – "Integration" – 'The Vital Ingredients'
Chapter 7 – "Where Next?" – 'Looking Ahead'

For the experienced coach who is already coaching a team and who is looking to develop greater expertise and also expand their sphere of influence I would recommend the following order:
Read from start to finish to identify with the logical progression of the chapters, or
Dip into the areas that need to be developed.

PREPARATION : THE HEART OF SUCCESS

There is no doubt in my mind that preparation is the heart of success. To just turn up and play and expect things to gel together is to be optimistic in the extreme, and yet that is what so often happens.

While everyone might not want to go along the path of Wolverhampton Cricket Club and their method of preparation, there will hopefully be ideas that will help make your team a better performing unit.

One of the early factors I recognised was that there are **eleven separate and quite distinct players who bring enormous diversity to the team.** Some have batting skills, some have bowling skills and some fielding or wicket keeping skills. Some bring at least two of these skills with them and in special cases perhaps even three.

Some batters are technically sound, others tactically sound, others mentally strong, others physically fit and others with excellent lifestyles. Some have several of the above and perhaps in a few, all of the above. The same can be said for bowlers, fielders and wicket keepers.

There is then the **support team** that are an essential part of the whole: the groundsman, the scorer, sometimes the umpire in Sunday games, the fixture secretary, the committee, the providers of refreshments, the person who runs the bar, the supporters and in some cases the parents.

The extended team are an essential part of the whole and need to be considered in preparation even though the lion's share of the skill of the coach is with helping to make the eleven players "tick" in a particular match and the squad "tick" over an entire season.

All of this is in the context of the appropriate profile for a coach to assume and this concludes chapter 6 (The Coach "Rising to the Challenge") where you are left with what is hopefully food for thought.

As coach, you are the eyes and ears of the club. The more you know about what is going on, the more likely you are to be able to act as a safety net. This puts you in a strong position to advise the chairman, club captain and selection committee in particular, and, where appropriate, intervene to reduce the conflicts that occur in every club.

The coach/player communication referred to in chapter 4 is not the only important communication issue of relevance to the coach. The issue of communication as an instrument by which the club is administered is also one in which the sensitive coach can assist. It's all about knowing when to stay quiet and when to intervene, but carefully handled, the coach can resolve many a problem before they surface.

One example is to do with selection. Players tend to get things "off their chests" to the coach when selection decisions and policies are disputed, and carefully expressed words from the coach in private to the chair of selectors can often bring information forward which would otherwise go unnoticed. This can often help resolve potential conflict.

This broader feel for what is meant by "preparation" is all the more important if the coach's role is to all playing members of the club, and not just the first team squad. In the case of Wolverhampton Cricket Club, this requires support for five regular Saturday teams and three Sunday teams together with a working knowledge of the quality players in the junior section who are available for selection.

Knowledge of the junior section is particularly important since it dovetails into the club coach's role. Regular contact with the chair of the junior section is very important, while making contact with as many as possible of the junior players during a season is also advocated. Taking special interest in those juniors who are in their last two or three years of junior membership pays dividends when these same youngsters step up into adult cricket. By way of helping the transition from junior to senior cricket, Wolverhampton has a policy whereby appropriate junior section players are invited to the senior coaching night.

But where does preparation start? If a coach is starting from scratch, it will differ from the established coach. There are, however, still many aspects that will be common.

It might sound self-evident, but I divide the year into three sections in terms of preparation:

- *Pre-season preparation*
- *During-the-season preparation*
- *Post-season preparation*

To provide some context, pre-season can start as early as January, while post-season can take up to Christmas to complete. Pre-season is characterised by increasing intensity, while the post-season is often associated with winding down, and focusing on 'where next'.

PRE-SEASON PREPARATION

Some of the following will seem self-evident, but are still included for completeness but often, reinforcing the obvious is an important part of developing good practice.

Winter nets/training needs to be booked well in advance. The decision as to what form this takes will depend on the priorities of the particular club. For some players this may be an opportunity for the sharpening of skills and technique, while for others it might be just a social event. The coach, on the other hand, will have physical and mental preparation on the list as well as technical development. Tactical and lifestyle issues will at this stage take a back seat, although lifestyle issues may well be dealt with on an individual basis, especially with first team squad members.

Once the decision has been made as to the type of preparation that is appropriate, it should be seen as a wise investment of time to make sure that players are well informed about the times and purpose of that practice. Communication for many clubs isn't the strongest aspect, so the coach can be a vital part of the communication loop. The contact with players on an individual basis helps form the building blocks upon which quality communication evolves and which over time effects performance on the pitch. Chapter 4 deals with this important issue in greater detail.

An important element of pre-season preparation for certain clubs is the recruitment of an **overseas player.** The coach will want to be involved in any discussions as to who this should be, or what skills that person needs to bring to the club. Therefore, advanced thought needs to be given to this issue.

If a club is considering an overseas player, then they should be fully aware of work permit regulations. The current position (2001) is that application has to be made to:

Department of Education and Employment,
Overseas Labour Service,
Sports and Entertainments Team,
W5 Moorfoot,
Sheffield,
S1 4PQ
Telephone: 0114 259 3710

The 2001 requirements to qualify for a work permit are that an overseas player needs to have evidence of playing either:

1. One "Test Match", or
2. Three "One-Day Internationals" or
3. Five "First Class" games in the country of their origin.

Overseas players (2001) must also be paid a minimum of £150 per week and be provided with accommodation. If a club wants an overseas player to do some coaching, then the player must hold a qualification that is recognised by the ECB. If they do not hold a recognised equivalent qualification, they must take the ECB Level II award prior to coaching actively.

Criteria review for overseas players seeking a work permit usually takes place annually and normally becomes available in January each year. Other ways of recruiting overseas players can be both illegal and risky.

This is not the place to make judgements about the common policy of employing overseas players. However, you may be interested to know that Wolverhampton decided on a policy for the year 2000 of trying to become self-sufficient after two years (1998 &1999) of using an overseas player to complement the existing strengths of the club first team squad. It was a bold strategy and I believe that if a club has a strong youth system, then the English game can only benefit from evidence of success at premier league levels without the dependence on an overseas player. In the ideal scenario, the very best young players will move into the "First Class" game and thereby make room for emerging talent.

As the introduction spelled out, Wolverhampton narrowly avoided relegation in the year without an overseas player and the trauma influenced the club to revert back to its former policy. This decision implies that it was the cause of the problem. As coach, I think this is making an excuse for the below standard performance of the team, but it's a complicated issue which is revisited in chapter 3 in the section "Vital Ingredient" - 'Mental'.

One of the reasons for the dependence on overseas or professional players in general in the UK, is our lack of forward planning at club level. Long-term preparation is required. Not only do we need to develop **youth policies** that develop technical competence in a variety of disciplines, but also policies that develop the mental skills that make us tougher to beat. Such ideas imply that "succession planning" has to be integral to the youth policy of a club, with all areas of the game being developed years ahead – batters (especially left-handers) and a variety of wrist and finger spinners and different types of seam/swing bowlers, not forgetting wicket keepers. The alternative, which the larger clubs can pursue, is attracting missing aspects from neighbouring clubs who play at a lower level. This should not amount to poaching but should ideally be part of good relationships with local clubs who recognise the benefit to the young player concerned. Some migration of young talent will take place anyway as talented youngsters seek opportunities at top clubs.

Grapevine gossip is an important part of the close season and the coach must be on the scent for changes that could well effect the preparation phase of a season. Routine contact with top players during the winter helps prevent approaches from other clubs who particularly thrive on the disaffection of players. The coach should be aware of which players are thinking of leaving or joining the club. There is no fool-proof system; only a good nose to pick up the scent and a good ear to pick up the hearsay! The captain and vice-captain of the first team should assist in this protection of the playing staff – the club's most valuable assets.

Keeping in touch is the important factor. It is connected to retaining the better players. Picking up the telephone to say, "how are you going?" is of value, but it is better for coach and player to meet to set an agenda for the next season as this provides the substance for follow-up telephone calls. It involves a player in their future development and galvanises their membership of what you want them to regard as "their" club. This process can be seen in the review system between player and coach, as described in chapter 4, and referred to it in chapter 3. In brief, the comprehensive review will involve the five essential elements of physical, mental, technical, tactical and lifestyle.

The immediate **pre-season timetable** and build up is the sharp end of a season's preparation. It needs to involve first team captain (and club captain if different), first team vice-captain, first team squad, practices and practice matches. If the first team's needs are met then the structure is likely to be of benefit to the whole club.

To help bring some of these ideas to life, outlined below is the pre-season timetable used at Wolverhampton Cricket Club.

Mid-March or earlier	a meeting with the first team captain to review the first team squad including who has left the club and who looks like joining. This is structured to provide a core of players divided into three columns: batters, bowlers and wicket keepers. If someone were an all-rounder then their name would feature in both batter and bowler columns. The same would apply to a wicket keeper/batter. For example:

Batters	Bowlers	Wicket Keepers
Captain	Captain	
Vice captain		
Batter "A"		
Batter "B"	Bowler "B"	
	Bowler "C"	
Wicket keeper "D"		Wicket Keeper "D"
	Etc.	

After starting the list with the captain and vice-captain, we add the other players in alphabetical order. Alphabetical order helps avoid hidden agendas being looked for by players.

The above list will be about 15-17 players who it is expected will form the nucleus of the squad. There may be some fringe players (say 3) who could fight their way in through good performances and they can be listed alphabetically after the main 17.

There is a final small list of players (say 3) that we call "long shots". These are players – some of whom may well be junior members – who it is thought have first team potential and who may get a first team opportunity on perhaps a Sunday or in a mid-week knock-out.

| **End March or earlier** | a meeting with the captain and vice-captain to discuss how the resources are going to be used tactically. Some consensus is desirable as to who is likely to be the first team along with possible batting orders and bowling combinations. This then leaves a good 4 weeks of thinking time to reflect on the views expressed. It starts to focus the mind of the captain, vice-captain and coach on the task ahead. |

The meeting can be structured in a similar way to the review for players. For example –

Where were we at the beginning of 2000?

What went well during 2000?

What would we like to improve?

What do we need to do to improve and to be ready for the 2001 season?

| **Early April** | a consultation meeting with players to discuss strategies and to agree what the priorities for the season ahead should be. This acts as the launching pad in the build up to the first league match. This, like the meeting with the captain and vice-captain, starts the vital process whereby the mental attribute of focus starts to become relevant to the players. |

An example of such a meeting can be found later in this chapter. The example is the one that was used at the beginning of the 1999 season following the winning of the "Birmingham and District Premier Cricket League" title in the inaugural year of 1998.

| **Early April or earlier** | a meeting with the chairman of the selection committee to discuss individual players, team squads, the identification of potential problem situations, basic administration management and a general tiptoe through the club politics. Isn't the political aspect common to all clubs? |

The chairman of selectors and the coach need to have a very good relationship and it is worth the time and effort to establish positive and confidential links. The coach can ask the questions which ensure that important issues have not been overlooked.

Examples of the sort of basic information that might be discussed would include the consideration of:

• *Match balls, scorebooks and availability chart (All of which should have been thought of a long time ago)*

- *League handbooks - several different leagues*
- *Changes to playing conditions, points systems, rules and regulations*
- *Club fixture card*
- *Knockout competitions and their rules (National and local)*
- *ECB directives*
- *Provisional team squads*
- *Potential "challenging" situations*

During April   a build up of practices and friendly matches, weather permitting, to acclimatise the players to grass after a winter of artificial surfaces and also to bring fielding into prominence. During this time, it is important to keep closely in touch with the groundsman, as there will almost inevitably be abandoned situations.

As far as practice is concerned I have found it useful to have an established procedure. The arrangement is that two nets will be set up. One will be on artificial, but the other will, if at all possible, be on grass. If I arrive and find the grass net is not set up and a second artificial net in its place, then this is the groundsman communicating with me that he feels it's too wet for a grass net. The organisation for a typical practice session can be found later on in this chapter.

An increase in **one-to-one contacts** is important during the build up to the start of the season. Each player is different and needs to be "tuned" to the task ahead. This does not have to be constructed formally, but reminders about issues previously discussed and agreed to be important can be raised without the player feeling threatened in any way. I believe that the role of the coach during this pre-season phase is to concentrate on the mental aspect of the players' preparation. The seriousness with which practice is conducted is a useful barometer of the mental state of any player. It's all about establishing the right balance between total dedication and commitment on one hand and enjoyment on the other.

TOOLS OF THE TRADE

Having all key information and equipment to hand can be a great time saver. Therefore, the coach would be well advised to create a lever arch file for all the necessary administration during March and April.

This was the content of my file for the 2000 season. Some of it will be unique to Wolverhampton, but it will hopefully trigger ideas that might be useful to coaches in other situations.

- Shift pattern for the season for captain and vice-captain (both police officers)
- Playing members telephone list
- Squad list for teams
- Opposition analysis sheet (see end of chapter, and chapter 5 – "Match Action").
- Attendance record for practices
- Practice admin: Net order, which players sign in as they arrive (see end of chapter)
- Practice admin: Bowling accuracy monitoring chart (see end of chapter).
- Agenda for 1st team squad pre-season meeting
- Agreed 1st team priorities
- New "Premier League" points system for 2000
- Important minutes from a winter "Premier League" meeting
- Copies of league registration forms - two separate leagues
- ECB "Fast Bowling Directives" 2000 version
- Copies of "Fast Bowling Directives" 2000 version for captains
- Information about junior section issues
- Fast bowler's known and anticipated cricketing commitments (see end of chapter)
- ECB safety guidance on the wearing of cricket helmets by young players
- Wolverhampton Cricket Club membership information
- Pre-season letters to members from the club chairman and club captain
- Agenda for March 2000 captains meeting
- Minutes for March 2000 captains meeting
- Administration for captains - Routines
- Club "Code of Conduct" including disciplinary procedures
- Rules and regulations for knockout competitions (Sunday and midweek).
- Personal notes on meeting with club captain re contractual issues
- Term of reference for "Club Coach" and "Personal Contract"
- Player reviews - original blank and completed version for players
- Other private information to do with first team squad members
- ECB "Wagon Wheels" for batting, bowling, fielding and wicket keeping (see end of chapter)
- 1999 averages and statistics.

In addition to the lever arch file, I carry a plastic box (13" x 9"). The arch lever file and A4 documents fit into it perfectly. Kept in this box are a number of "essentials" that either will or might be needed for a match. Included for 2000 were the following:

- The 2000 lever arch file including the information listed above

- The 1999 lever arch file
- Hardback clip folder for "Match of the Day" information
- 2000 diary
- Individual file for each opposition side
- 1999 individual files of each opposition side
- Handbooks for leagues (Saturdays & Sundays)
- ECB "Regulations and Playing Conditions" handbook
- The Laws of Cricket
- Spare copies of "Opposition Analysis" sheets
- Spare copies of "Net Order" sheet for practice night
- Spare copies of "Bowling Accuracy Monitoring Charts" for practice night
- Spare copies of "Bowling Monitoring Form" - known and anticipated commitments
- Team selection book for all sides for Saturdays and Sundays
- Several Bic master pencils
- Several biros
- Spare A4 paper
- Calculator
- Umpires 'ball and over counter'
- "Visual Acuity Chart" for vision testing
- Bank bag for collecting valuables during matches
- Mobile phone.

Separately I carry the following in a cricket "equipment" bag, which is used on practice nights and during the warm up for matches:
- Two sets of "Kwik" cricket in two purpose designed bags
- Bat (normal), narrow bat (3" wide) and mini bat for catching (24" long)
- Bat handle cone for bat handle grips.

In addition I carry the following in a large "Rumble Trunk" (32"x16"):
- First aid kit (Small) for use during matches on commonplace injuries. (It includes amongst other things ice-spray, muscle rub, plasters, paracetamol {for adult players only}, and a surgical glove for when blood is involved).
- The smaller plastic box with all the day-to-day contents (as above)
- A bag of fielding/catching leather balls
- A baseball mitt
- 3 boxes of 4 leather balls (1 two-coloured) in 3 plastic sandwich boxes with lid.
- 6 incrediballs or similar for use in cold weather

(Esp. early season)
- Small cones for marking an area out for warm-up purposes
- Two spare quality balls for emergency purposes during a match
- One "new" ball for an emergency occasion
- Plastic carton of chalk
- Separately: first aid kit (Holdall) for more complicated injuries.

I also carry the following injury pack in a "freezer" box:
- 4 x frozen ice packs
- 4 x 2 litre used milk cartons full of cold water
- A damp cloth for use in treating bruises and e.g. cut eyes
  to staunch the flow
- 3 Freezer pads for use within damp cloth.

And finally, a pantechnicon to carry it all in (only joking) but a hatch-back helps. At home, there are a few other resources that may be used on specific occasions. Included in this list would be a 'Speedcheck' machine, which can record the speed of a bowler's delivery and a bowler's strap, which can help co-ordinate the arms in a bowler's delivery.

Example of a Pre-season Players' Meeting (April 1999)

Prior to contacting players, the mid-March meeting with the captain was used to determine the anticipated squad for the season. Having established this, the best date for the first team meeting was discussed with some key players. Fifteen players from a squad of seventeen were able to attend. The meeting took place in the clubhouse, and a circular seating arrangement chosen. If consultation is the intention, then a circle is far more interactive than rows of chairs. A flip-chart was used to record the key details of the meeting.

I set the agenda by asking a central question. **"What have we got to do to replicate the success of the 1998 season?"** The following process was then followed.

1. Two groups were formed to discuss the question. The captain and vice-captain had been asked prior to the meeting to lead the discussion with a group (10minutes).

2. Players were then asked to pair up and to discuss the question further and to come up with what they thought were 5 important factors. (5 minutes approximately) I just listened in and moved round the pairs.

3. In turn, each pair was asked to state their 5 factors. The result was a list of 17 factors, which were posted on the flip chart.

4. The 17 factors were discussed as a whole group. The players who had suggested a factor made supplementary comments when requested to expand the point they were trying to make. Players were encouraged to

challenge any factor if they thought it not very important. This discussion clarified issues.

5. Players then went back into their pairs to respond to a request to prioritise what they thought were the main factors, which would lead to a repetition of success. They were asked to pick their top 5 from 17.

6. The choices were placed on the flip chart with a point given for each selection.

7. The outcome was a long list with the number of selections alongside. The top 5 scores became the priorities of the team.

OUR AGREED PRIORITIES

TEAM SPIRIT
WORKING IN UNITS

PREPARATION
TRAINING / PRACTICE

MENTAL STRENGTH
(Toughness)

FOCUS
(Concentration)

ENJOYMENT

The above information was then presented on A4 paper, posted in the dressing room and referred to when appropriate.

After the players had decided the above priorities, I added my "two pennyworth" in a premeditated addition: that every player and the coach had a duty to establish contact with everyone else in the squad. I presented this idea visually as 12 dots in a circle, which were all connected to each other. See the diagram below.

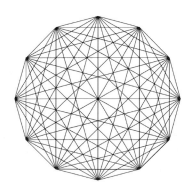

I suggested that it was this that would give us a team strength, which was more than the sum of our individual parts, and that it would be this that would hold us together in times of crisis. An example of this happening can be found in the match against Farnworth in the 1999 National Knock-out last 16 match when Wolverhampton were 27 for 5 and yet still reached the target of 164 for the loss of 8 wickets. This example is expanded upon in Chapter 4.

Factors to consider in the preparation for "Practice" before and during the season.

It has already been mentioned earlier that it is important to keep closely in touch with the groundsman and to have agreed arrangements. These are particularly valuable when the weather is poor. The groundsman, however, is not the only important cog in the practice arena.

The fixture secretary is another person with whom close contact needs to be maintained. Not only will forward planning have gone into the quantity and quality of pre-season friendly matches, but also into quickly arranged fixture bureaux matches when opposition teams "cry off" at short notice.

We are lucky in the Midlands in this respect to have such a service available. A request for the fixture secretary to keep you in the communication loop with a quick telephone call to ensure you know what is going on pays immeasurable dividends. There are also many knockout matches during a season and the fixture secretary is often the first point of contact. While practice night is generally avoided, fixture congestion does not always allow the night to remain free. An early warning about a match can help organisation and preparation.

In addition to senior knockout matches, Wolverhampton has a sophisticated and well-organised junior section that plays in excess of 130 matches a season. Most of them are in the evenings and Sunday morning and many have to be re-arranged at short notice during inclement weather. So established procedures and thorough preparation as to how to organise practice and also enable a junior (or senior) cricket match to proceed is vital.

On a rare occasion, both squares could be used with perhaps a senior match on one and a junior match on the other. In these circumstances, it is again vital that the coach is thoroughly prepared beforehand with established procedures and a strategy as to how to make the most of the situation. Artificial strips that are designed such that they can be set up outside the boundary area provide a lifeline in such situations. The same care would still be required in a one square club. Flexibility in planning is essential.

The bar person is another person who needs to know about cancellations and rearrangements if time and money are not to be wasted. The coach can act as an informal vehicle for communication. It's rather like providing an early warning system about known or potential hazards.

The goodwill that can be established by showing consideration for the position of the groundsman, fixture secretary, junior chairman and bar person, especially in the unpredictable early season, is an absolute must for the thinking coach.

DURING-THE-SEASON PREPARATION

A "Typical" Practice Session

Checklists of what equipment is needed and what facilities are required can save a lot of time.

Example of equipment:
- 3 sandwich boxes (with lids to keep balls dry) of 4 x 5½ oz cricket balls
- 1 yellow and red leather ball included in each box
- 6 incrediballs for use in cold weather
- Bag of softer fielding and catching leather balls
- Small cones (for warm ups and also to indicate fielders in simulated practices);
- 2 sets of "kwik" cricket stumps
- Coach's bat
- "Thin" bat (3" wide) for specialist batters and shadow work for wicket keepers
- "Mini" bat for catching practice
- "Shower" mat for wicket keeping practice off an uneven surface
- Bowling machine and associated balls
- Plastic carton of chalk
- First aid kit
- Mobile telephone
- Water to prevent dehydration.

Example of facilities that might be arranged (as mentioned earlier a consistent routine helps communication with the groundsman and helps reduce misunderstandings):
- 1 grass net on the square
- 1-2 artificial wickets. The second would replace the grass wicket in poor weather;
- 1 artificial wicket/strip for use with the bowling machine
- An area to perform fielding drills.

The positional arrangement of facilities is important to the effectiveness of the coach. At Wolverhampton, for example, we have two squares, and to have an arrangement of one artificial net on one square and another net on grass on the other means that the coach is bouncing from one place to another with a distance of about 100metres between each. A better arrangement is to have both nets (one artificial + one grass) on one square and to have another area for fielding not too far away. This allows the coach to quickly transfer his/her attention to each of the nets and to the fielding group. Whatever the facilities, the coach is well advised to devise a routine for making the most of what is available and to ensure that the players understand the thinking behind the organisation.

I run the practice on my own with the help of senior players on occasions. They help with the fielding practices, in particular, so organisation is vital. Ideally it would be helpful if the same senior players were available each week, as this would allow more detailed planning.

This is my basic organisation:

- I arrive approximately 30-45 minutes before the start of the practice
- Take the "Rumble" trunk (mentioned earlier) and cricket "equipment" bag to a set area where players congregate
- Assemble the "kwik" cricket sets
- Assemble the bowling machine (Set up for a right arm over bowler bowling to right hand batter at about 60 mph as a starting base line, from which adjustments can be made to speed, length, line and trajectory) Try to arrange for someone else to arrive early to help.
- Place the "Net Order" sheet (see end of chapter) in a prominent place for players to sign-up for a net order in either grass/artificial or machine nets (described below).

The agenda for the practice is connected to the performance in the previous league match for the first team and to the individual performance of players. This means that mental, technical and tactical aspects are likely to be prominent. For players in other teams, the agenda will be more technical and mental, although tactical matters can be discussed.

In the ideal world, I would like the following:

- Practice to involve several appointed coaches and for each squad to work independently with their own coach for a significant amount of time each week. Overlap is inevitable and desirable and would require coordination between the coaches. (There would be plenty of opportunity for different squads to share activities, e.g., fielding drills.)
- A culture and expectation that all squad members would attend unless there were very good reasons otherwise.
- An organisation that would allow rotation of players in well-constructed

groups with each group being led by a specialist coach.
- For there to be a net component, a fielding component and a one-to-one discussion/review/debrief/feedback/development component based on the previous match
- For specific group practice sessions to be arranged, outside the above organisation, for specific purposes.

Example 1   The batters to work as a group on, say, the "sweep" or on "moving out to drive and then defend, hit along the ground or hit over the top".

Example 2   The finger spin bowlers to work as a group on, say, developing the arm ball and "floater".

Example 3   The pace bowlers working on taking a return catch immediately after the delivery of a ball. (This would be a simulated practice. Other examples can be found in the technical section of chapter 3.)

The above practices and other specific group practices would emphasise not only technique but also the tactical "when" of their application.

The reality at Wolverhampton Cricket Club is that there are not the financial resources to service such a system although some of the above specific practices can be incorporated. The coach is available to all club members on one night of the week only. One-to-one discussions have to take place as and when they can be arranged. Some can be done on the practice night but much has to take place on the telephone, on match days, evening knockouts, or whenever the opportunity can be found. The coach also needs to make him/herself approachable and accessible, almost on demand, as many of the non-first team players would other-wise be deprived of advice and contact with the coach.

The reality is that many amateur players regard practice as desirable and not compulsory or vital. The full squad rarely attend as a total unit and so the skill of the coach is to dovetail all the bits and pieces into a coherent whole. This means that the important dialogue between players is missing except on match days when the circumstances don't always lend themselves to debate! Sometimes, especially when things are not going according to plan, it is the team meeting that can pave the way to improvement.

The coach must plan on the basis of doing it on his own and be flexible enough to use senior players as and when the opportunity arises.

Planning for practice can take place in general terms but needs to change according to the numbers that turn up on a particular night and the team composition represented.

The ideal referred to earlier may come over time but we are a long way off reaching the culture of expectation that exists in say an Australian first grade top club side where intensity in practice is the norm and where quality is more important than quantity. However, it is a goal to set, a goal to work towards and a standard to which we should aspire.

My own planning for practice is always looking for ways to improve, and in chapter 6 - "The Coach - Rising to the Challenge", this philosophy underpins my approach to personal development.

"ROUTINE" OR "NORMAL" PRACTICE EVENING

Running a practice session after a good performance is a relatively easy affair, because the players are less likely to attend carrying "baggage" from the weekend, although in every match there will be players who will have succeeded and players who will perceive themselves to have failed. The chapter on communication deals with the ways in which players need to be handled differently following a weekend of cricket based on their success or perceived lack of it.

The current practice arrangements work quite well and include the following general pattern:

• As players arrive, they sign the "Net Order" chart (see end of chapter) to say whether and when they want to bat and if so, which of the two alternatives they prefer.

a) Working with a partner using the bowling machine on specific front or back foot play for approximately 30 minutes, (sometimes in 3's and sometimes using an injured player to "feed") or,

b) Batting 7 minutes on grass followed by 7 minutes on artificial with a 1 minute transfer time between the two nets This allows for combinations of circumstances to be created: e.g., 7 minutes against spin and 7 minutes against medium/quick, on one or other of the surfaces in order to demand adaptability and flexibility in the way batters bat.

The element of choice implied above doesn't mean that the coach is unable to influence what a particular player concentrates on at a particular practice, but it does give the coach a flavour of the mood of the player.

• Because players arrive at different times, the first batter usually gets 15 minutes on grass, but as soon as there are enough players, both the grass and artificial nets are used, and a rotation created (e.g., for option (b) above).

	Grass	Changeover	Artificial
Batter 1	6.05pm (15 mins)		
Batter 2	6.20pm (7 mins)	6.27pm (1 min)	6.28pm (7 mins)
Batter 3	6.27pm (7 mins)	6.34pm (1 min)	6.35pm (7 mins)
Batter 4	6.34pm (7 mins)	6.41pm (1 min)	6.42pm (7 mins)

• As more bowlers arrive, I try to pair them up according to "type". Off spinners together, if possible, but using left arm orthodox if necessary to keep finger spin together. Spin combinations are always used in preference to a spin bowler and a quicker bowler combination. Wrist spinners would be paired, as too would medium/quick bowlers whenever possible etc.

• The pairs of bowlers bowl, whenever possible, in 6-ball over spells, so if two pairs were working in a net, they would alternate, two on, two off. This is better for the batter because they get some consistent style of deliveries and it's good for the bowlers because it simulates a game situation. (It's also good for young fast bowlers working to the "ECB Fast Bowling Directives", as it is easier for them to keep count of the number of deliveries in a particular practice if their workload is calculated in overs.)

• This structure allows the coach to intervene at any point to set up a "match situation" which can be particularly challenging to the batter or to the bowler or to both, depending on whether the coach shares the information with one or both party's. The "match situation" can often relate to the previous match while the experience is still fresh.

• This structure also allows the coach to use the "Bowling accuracy monitoring charts" (included at the end of this chapter).

• When enough players have arrived to service both nets and to leave spare capacity, the fielding group is started. If the specialist senior player is available, I leave him to it, but in his absence I suggest (maybe set up) what activities should be practised, start it off and then rotate between nets and fielding practice. The players know a selection of practices from previous occasions and can usually organise the drills with a small amount of intervention from the coach. The coach's role is usually to demand high standards and to motivate as the performance skill threshold of a particular practice is designed to be within the grasp of all of the participants.

The above structure is used in what I call a "normal" or " routine" practice evening, but on occasions after a poor league performance, the practice can be modified (see below).

The ECB Level II course, "Working in Nets", expands the ideas concerning types of net that can be run. Again the imagination of the coach is required to pick the most appropriate for a particular practice.

Example 1   An "Analysis Net" where bowlers enter into a discussion after bowling an over or two at a batter to discuss strengths and weaknesses observed. This type of net develops the ability of the bowlers to analyse in match situations.

Example 2   A "Running Net" where there are two batters and four bowlers and after each shot the coach shouts the number of runs scored and the batters run them. This would include quick singles and well-driven 3's.

Example 3   A dismissed net where a batter can be out bowled, LBW, caught, and caught and bowled. This encourages the placement of a value on a batters wicket and an incentive for the bowlers to try and get people out.

There are others, which are covered during the ECB Level II course, some stopping just short of an actual game.

The above may give the impression that 'practice equals nets plus fielding' plus specific skill development. This is not the case. Sometimes it is more appropriate to have a "square practice" in order to improve for example, running between the wickets, taking short singles, stopping short singles, and backing up procedures. Sometimes a "square practice" can form part of an evening practice.

Changes in Circumstances which alter the "Routine" or "Normal" Practice.

There are a number of situations which arise that require flexibility in the organisation of a practice evening. The following are examples that alter the numbers attending:

X Inclement weather

X Work commitments

X Altered night following, for example, a Public Holiday

X Holidays

X Knock-out competition commitments, especially when poor weather causes a backlog of matches

I believe that in England (certainly the West Midlands) we play too many mid-week knockout matches. As a generalisation, I would say that we play too much cricket and practice too little, but the facts are that knockout matches bring players to the club and increase the turnover of the bar, which for many clubs is their financial lifeline.

A coach can try to argue the case for less mid-week cricket, but it's one of the uncontrollable factors that coaches have to learn to live with. The above 5 points are also out of the control of the coach.

Rather than moan about the smaller numbers in one of these situations, I regard it as an opportunity to make the practice session more interesting and more specifically moulded to fit the needs of the players that attend.

Examples of how limited numbers can be made to work for, rather than against, would include the following:

a) A young first team batter had a poor performance against spin in a recent league match and looked to have little confidence and no apparent strategy. On the same occasion, there were three off spin bowlers present who had played first team cricket at some time.

A game like situation was set up in the net, which was designed to explore strategies that the left-handed bat could employ. The bowlers were just asked to bowl in overs as if it was a game.

The batter was left to start with so that I could analyse what his thinking process appeared to be. I moved in (standing behind the net) when it became apparent that there was no real strategy at work, no method.

To start with, he would play a shot and I would ask what the purpose of the shot selection was. Other questions like "Which way was the ball spinning", "Was that an arm ball?", "Would that have been a risky shot" etc. would follow.

I would then set a classic field and use markers to indicate the positions of the fielders and then tell him how I would approach one of the three bowlers, a tall bowler who delivered from about 10 feet high. I would tell him what to do and he would try to execute the advice. e.g. "Move down the wicket and play a defensive shot unless you are really over the top of the ball - i.e. a "big" half volley", or "Stay in your crease and let the ball complete more of its flight before deciding what shot to play" etc. This would be my attempt to indicate that there are several ways in which spin can be approached. The bowler must not be allowed to conclude that you are predictable. The bowler has to be set problems otherwise his job is made easier.

Once a few strategies had been introduced, the player would then be left to try and develop their own.

b) A first team off spin bowler who bowls well generally but finds it difficult to respond when the opposition "take him on" and attack.

I would arrange, if possible before the practice evening, for an experienced attacking batsman who is capable of destroying an opposition bowler to co-operate in the practice. There are two ways in which the practice could be set up. The scene would be set in either a net on a one-to-one basis (bowler and bat) and the coach, or on a pitch on the square with fielders to simulate as realistic a situation as possible.

Again, the coach explores strategies for combating the attacking approach of the batter and then leaves the bowler to try and work out their own.

The above are but examples. The only limitation is the imagination of the coach to set up game like situations that are specific to individual players.

Practice Evening following a poor performance

Sometimes it might have been the batting that lacked cohesion, sometimes it might have been the bowling that hadn't been accurate enough while sometimes it might have been the fielding that was poor overall in say catching. Less frequently it might be more than one of the above or for it to be bits of each.

If I thought that the performance of the first team catching was below standard, I might, for example, set the evening up as normal, but start with a discussion between players where non first team players would be invited to listen. I would ask the non-first team players to agree to join us in a catching practice first, so that the "ghost" of the match could be put to rest. Where harsh words were needed, I would deal with this quickly at the beginning of the practice in order that a constructive phase could be entered into.

From a personal point of view, it is precisely after a disappointing performance that players need to have their game developed. In these circumstances I try to be creative and coach something new. I find this far more beneficial than dwelling on something that went wrong.

Generally speaking, I find that poor performance is seldom to do with lack of ability. It is sometimes to do with the inexperience of a player or the team, but most often the cause is connected with the mental approach of a player or the team.

The most important thing in a practice after a poor performance is to re-establish confidence. The challenges set by the coach should reflect that objective and try to build confidence by setting challenges that increase in small steps of difficulty. Pushing too hard can frequently increase anxiety levels and lead to mistakes, and have the opposite effect. A coach must be prepared to modify previously agreed targets if this is appropriate to the restoration of confidence. It is a skilful judgement to make.

Team activities are also often more fruitful than concentrated individual attention. If a player needs to work of an aspect that is causing a persistent problem, then success is often better established in a one-to-one situation (see below) and not in front of lots of other players, although this depends on the individual player.

One-to-one Practices

Occasionally players need to work on a one-to-one basis. This could be for any area of the game: e.g., physical fitness, mental toughness, technical batting, bowling, fielding or wicket keeping, tactical awareness or lifestyle. Sometimes it will be a practical session while on others it will involve only discussion. If the reason for the practice is to overcome a difficulty, this is best achieved by holding a one-to-one private coaching session. (Be aware of 'Child Protection' issues if this involves a young player. See chapter 6 for more information.)

Pair and small group practices

On occasions, it is appropriate to work in pairs or in small groups. This could involve just the seam bowlers, or just the spin bowlers, or all the bowlers and all the batters, etc. Sometimes this might be to work on technique, sometimes on combined strategies between pairs of bowlers, sometimes on specialist fielding positions, sometimes on developing the mental side of the game, etc.

Preparation for matches

Chapter 5 deals with this in detail where a case study is made of preparation for Birmingham and District Premier Cricket League matches and separately of preparation for ECB National Club Championship matches. Also included in chapters 3 and 5 is reference to footwear for batters, bowlers and fielders, sunglasses and skin protection as well as the issues of dehydration and energy depletion.

Post-season preparation

While this is generally the quiet time, there are occasions when issues need to be resolved. This could be with individuals, with a team or club players meeting, with captain or captain and vice-captain etc. An example of post-season activity can be found in chapter 5 in the case study on avoiding relegation from the Birmingham and District Premier Cricket League.

As a final thought, while preparation is undoubtedly the "Heart of Success", it alone is not the sole determinant of success.

USING THE WAGON WHEEL

The purpose of the "Wagon Wheel" is to give you a clear picture of how you see yourself in the various disciplines of the game.

The centre of each "wheel" represents "0" and the rim represents "10".
Rate yourself (honestly!) out of 10 in each segment: "0" = very weak; "10" = as good as you can be.

Shade in the appropriate segment to the necessary level, e.g.

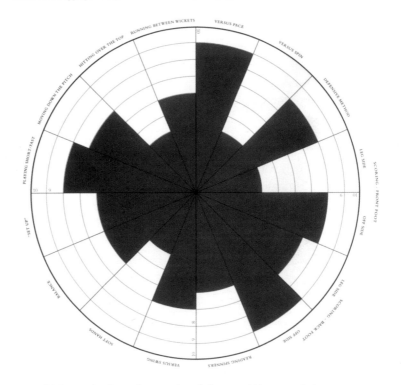

This will help you identify your key strengths and also areas which may require improvement.
Your short term goal may be to improve by perhaps one level, e.g. 5 to 6 in one or more segments.
Your medium to long term goal should be to create a more symmetrical profile, indicating polished all round skills.

R.C. LOG WW

WICKET KEEPING

CRICKETER:	DATE:
SQUAD:	COACH:

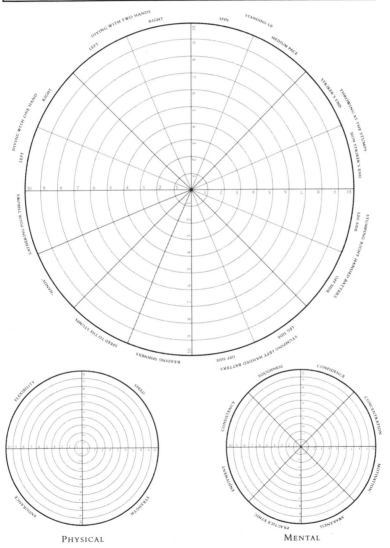

PHYSICAL

MENTAL

RC LOG WKT

BATTING

CRICKETER:	DATE:
SQUAD:	COACH:

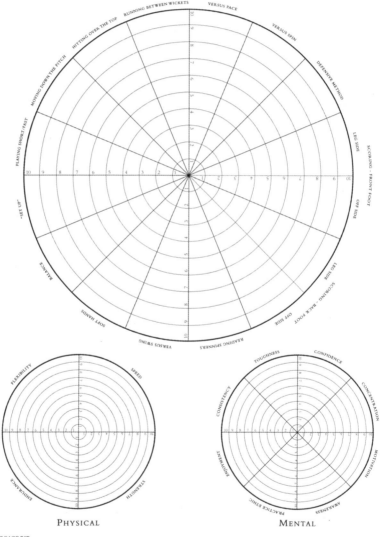

PHYSICAL

MENTAL

RC LOG BAT

BATTING AGAINST SPIN

CRICKETER:	DATE:
SQUAD:	COACH:

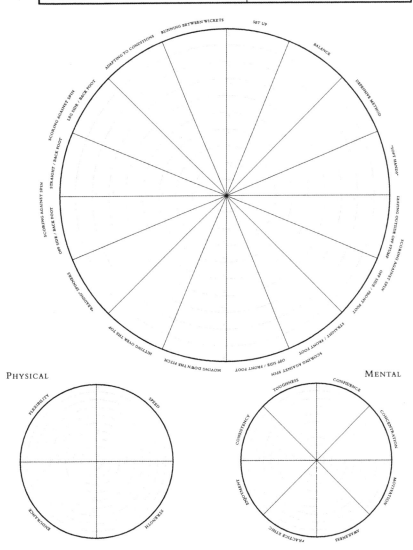

PHYSICAL

MENTAL

BATTING AGAINST PACE

CRICKETER:	DATE:
SQUAD:	COACH:

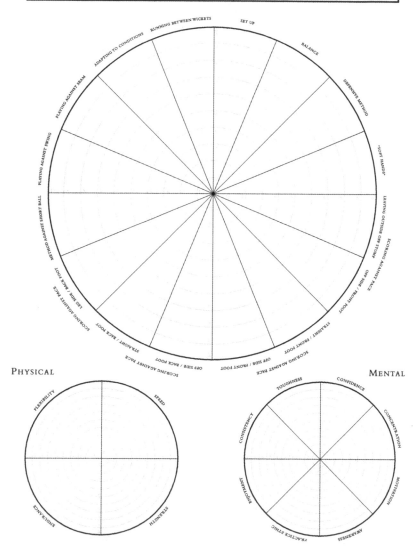

PHYSICAL

MENTAL

BOWLING – SPIN

CRICKETER:	DATE:
SQUAD:	COACH:

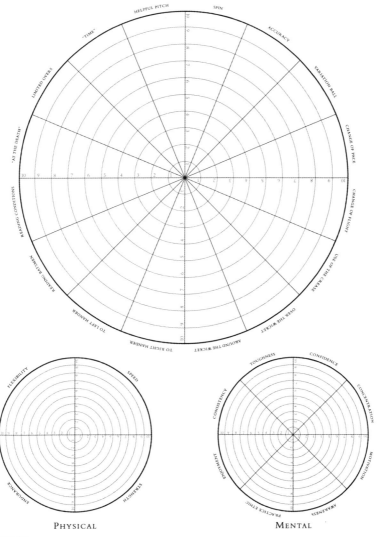

PHYSICAL

MENTAL

RC LOG BWL-S

BOWLING - PACE

NATIONAL CRICKET · COACH INITIATIVE · ECB

CRICKETER:	DATE:
SQUAD:	COACH:

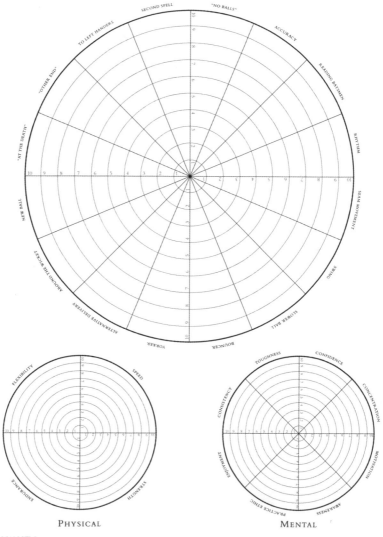

PHYSICAL

MENTAL

RC LOG BWL-P

"OPPOSITION ANALYSIS SHEET"

DATE............ OPPONENTS...

OVERALL COMMENT...
....

KEY OPPOSITION TARGETS...
....

Position in table.....	P	W	Wd	Ld	L	Aban	Bon	Pts

Overall record...

Last five matches..

AGAINST
& RESULT......... 1 .... 2 .... 3 .... 4 .... 5 ....

SCORES...

BATTING

1 ....
2 ....
3 ....
4 ....
5 ....
6 ....

Comments
Rate/aver etc..

BOWLING

1 ....
2 ....
3 ....
4 ....
5 ....
6 ....

Comments
Strike rate/econ/aver..

NET ORDER

DATE.............

LIVE NET ON ARTIFICIAL / GRASS   **MACHINE**

1................................   1................................

2................................   2................................

3................................   3................................

4................................   4................................

5................................   5................................

6................................   6................................

7................................   7................................

8................................   8................................

9................................   9................................

10................................   10................................

BOWLING ACCURACY MONITORING CHART

Name............................   Age.........   Action.................

FOR RIGHT HANDED BATTERS

1.1	1.2	1.3	1.4	1.5	1.6

2.1 7	2.2 8	2.3 9	2.4 10	2.5 11	2.6 12

3.1	3/2	3.3	3.4	3.5	3.6

4.1	4.2	4.3	4.4	4.5	4.6

5.1	5.2	5.3	5.4	5.5	5.6

6.1	6.2	6.3	6.4	6.5	6.6

1.1	1.1	1.1	1.1	1.1	1.1

BOWLING ACCURACY MONITORING CHART

Name.............................. Age......... Action..................

FOR LEFT HANDED BATTERS

| 1.1 | 1.2 | 1.3 | 1.4 | 1.5 | 1.6 |

| 2.1 7 | 2.2 8 | 2.3 9 | 2.4 10 | 2.5 11 | 2.6 12 |

| 3.1 | 3/2 | 3.3 | 3.4 | 3.5 | 3.6 |

| 4.1 | 4.2 | 4.3 | 4.4 | 4.5 | 4.6 |

| 5.1 | 5.2 | 5.3 | 5.4 | 5.5 | 5.6 |

| 6.1 | 6.2 | 6.3 | 6.4 | 6.5 | 6.6 |

| 1.1 | 1.1 | 1.1 | 1.1 | 1.1 | 1.1 |

WOLVERHAMPTON CRICKET CLUB

**BOWLING MONITORING FORM (especially fast bowlers)
FOR KNOWN AND ANTICIPATED CRICKETING COMMITMENTS**

NAME........................ TELEPHONE NUMBER...............

WEEK BEGINNING MONDAY........./........./ 2001

TYPE OF GAME (E.g., 2-day, 1-day (50 over), 20 over K.O.)

Day of week	Date	Where	Type of game	County (Co) Club (Cl) School (Sch)
Monday				
Tuesday				
Wednesday				
Thursday				
Friday				
Saturday				
Sunday				

Other comments (E.g., Coursework schedules, examination commitments, school and family holidays)

....
....

Complete the diary sheet weekly and remember to enter on the availability chart what you believe your availability to be bearing in mind the ECB directives. Ask Arthur Pickering or John Moore if you are not sure. Keep your records so that you can be monitored. This is essential for fast bowlers, and desirable for all bowlers.

RECORD FROM PREVIOUS WEEK ~
WEEK ENDING SUNDAY........./........./ 2001

	Mon	Tues	Wed	Thur	Fri	Sat	Sun
OVERS							
SPELLS							
MATCHES							

ACCUMULATED TOTALS

	Mon	Tues	Wed	Thur	Fri	Sat	Sun	TOTAL
OVERS								
SPELLS								
MATCHES								

Other comments (from player or parent/guardian/carer)...........

....

INTEGRATION : THE VITAL INGREDIENTS

The vital ingredients are not new – they have been around for a long time. Perhaps the difference is that more is known as to how they interact and how to bring them together as a whole.

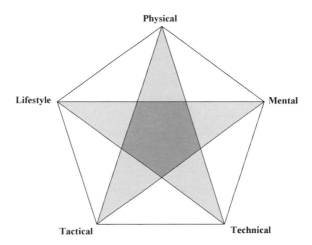

It was mentioned in the introduction that this book was about none and yet all of the above ingredients, and it was mentioned in the previous chapter that members of a team or squad bring a vast variety of expertise and competence concerning the above factors for the coach to consider.

The essential thing for the coach is to have some knowledge about all of the above and be able to advise. Short of that, it is to know in which areas you will need to ask for help or refer for guidance. To know where to go for the appropriate information is vital. Also vital is to acknowledge that you don't know it all and to recognise that accepting this reality is strength and not weakness. The higher the quality of the player you are dealing with, the more readily should the coach seek advice from specialists.

In working with players, the coach will benefit if he/she views the above five ingredients within the background of an emotional state of mind of both player and coach. Both parties can bring different moods to any situation dependent on their personal circumstances. While a professional approach to coaching will enable the coach to overcome personal difficulties, the same might not be true for the player. Ways of working therefore need to be flexible with adjustments made for personal circumstances. All coaches who enrol on an ECB Level I Coaching Course receive a manual as part of their course fee to which is added supplementary material for Level II and Level III. The manual and the supplementary material contain a lot of very important information for the aspiring coach. In the following five sections on physical, mental, technical, tactical and lifestyle, frequent reference will be made to the "ECB Cricket Coach's Manual" which will be called "Coach's Manual" for short. See next page for a diagram of the "New Coaching Scheme".

In each of the five areas, there will be less of an emphasis on downloading information to the reader, but more on ways in which I have used information to improve the performance of individual players and through this the performance of the team. It's more a case of examples of a way of working than a comprehensive and all-embracing text.

A coach doesn't need a library of books to be well prepared. What is more important is that there are a few sources of information, which succinctly get to the heart of what you want to know. Coaches are busy people who, without loss of quality, need short cuts wherever possible.

There is a bibliography at the end of the book. It is not extensive because I don't believe it needs to be. It can be added to, however, as coaches develop expertise in the various "ingredients". My own library is larger, but the purpose of this book is to keep things simple and to help coaches to get started. The more advanced coaches will be able to integrate their own sources of information into their own strategy.

For the aspiring coach, however, who has no qualifications at the moment, there is no better way to "get started" than working through the ECB Coaching Scheme.

The central sources of information that I use in this section are:

1. The "ECB Cricket Coach's Manual"
2. "Play Better Cricket" by Stephen J. Bull et al
3. "The Mental Game Plan" by Stephen J. Bull et al

The above books will be referred to by title only in order to avoid repetition.

PHYSICAL

Wolverhampton Cricket Club has a young side and fitness has not been made a priority in the terms of reference of the coach. The coach, however, needs to be able to advise on the development of a number of fitness components including: endurance, strength, speed, and flexibility to which could be added power and agility. There is advice on these areas in an ECB Level II course as well as supplementary material added to the "Coach's Manual". The first four areas also feature in the wagon wheel approach to the profiling of what level a player perceives their current status to be on a 1-10 point scale. See examples at the end of chapter two.

The ECB have recently distributed an "ECB Performance Diary" (1) for the use of all county under 13, 15, 17 and 19 age groups. They contain

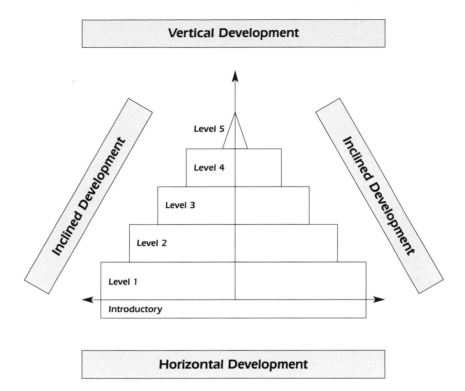

Vertical development – enables a coach to progress sequentially through the **National Coaching Scheme** levels

Inclined development or "bridging courses" – courses provide relevant information to facilitate and encourage vertical progression

Available from 1st September 2001

Horizontal development – Courses provide relevant information targeted at coaches who are content at their present level, but who wish to remain "current".
The courses may create aspiration towards inclined development.

Available from 1st September 2001

a lot of useful information. The Under 15 Diary, for example, gives a succinct yet clear rationale for players being physically fit when it states that being physically fit will help to:

- Keep up your expected skill levels
- Recover from exertion more quickly
- Reduce the risk of injury
- Reduce physical and mental tiredness
- Keep your concentration
- Bat, bowl, field & keep wicket longer
- Give you an edge over the opposition

And the above are no less valid for older players over the age of 15!

I believe that the enlightened coach will not only be aware of the above benefits but also know the correct way to warm up, stretch, exercise/practice/play, warm down and stretch again. The enlightened coach will be specifically aware of the dangers to fast bowlers of not being physically prepared, of having inappropriate footwear, of having technical imperfections (e.g., mixed action) and simply doing too much bowling.

The ECB Level III course provides significant information in physical preparation for cricket including training principles and cricket specific circuit training.

The coach, ideally, also needs to know how to devise with individual players a programme for the year, which integrates physical, mental, technical, tactical and lifestyle management issues. Planning a programme is an integral part of an ECB Level III course. There is a summary of this process written by Nigel Stockill in the *Association of Cricket Coaches Journal No. 28*, December 1998 (2), in which he talks about being fit for cricket, the need to plan, periodisation (divided into transition, preparatory and competition phases), testing and progression.

All of the above doesn't happen overnight. It is necessary to start small and build from there. Keep it simple and develop experience with players who are keen to "work at it". Some players in the Wolverhampton first team squad are not pre-disposed to hard work during the winter for example, and think it is "too late" for them, but the younger players want to be challenged and pushed along. It's a case of horses for courses. Gradually over a few years, more of the squad will subscribe to the benefits of an all-round planned physical programme, especially if development in technical, tactical, mental and lifestyle management issues are added as part of a whole personal development plan. As a coach, plan not just for the present and near future, but for that vision of the future that you hope to create.

In a simple form, coaches who haven't been on a Level III course can recognise the need to plan in advance for the phases even if the detail is in far less depth. For example, it makes logical sense to consider the following phases:

- To rest at the end of a season and to do alternative recreational activities

- To work on general and then more specific training over the main winter months in identified areas of need

- To follow this with even more specific pre-season work

- And finally to maintain a level of fitness throughout the season.

Dealing with this bit-by-bit while knowledge develops can still be very important although guesswork and advice based on hearsay is perhaps not a good idea! It's not advisable for a coach to pose and act as if they are highly knowledgeable if they are not. The confidence of the team will disappear overnight if you do. Accept your limitations and work within them, while you develop your expertise. In the final analysis, there is no substitute for "knowing your stuff".

In deciding what to work on, I recommend that this is not downloaded to adult players but made part of a review process which leads to the shared identification of areas of need. Even then it will only be appropriate for some players. You can't force things onto amateur players, only persuade. Some of the things I have helped players with, following discussion, include:

- Running style and correct use of the arms

- Distribution of weight when running so that acceleration is effective

- Using lampposts for shuttle running to develop speed between the wickets

- Using the perimeter of the Wolverhampton ground as a set distance over which to measure timed performance when developing endurance

- Recommending that basic workout routines are followed each week in the off season e.g., a minimum of 3 x 20 minutes workouts if improved cardio-vascular endurance is the objective

- Supporting players during the off season who express a wish to maintain their level of fitness

- Advising on the undesirability of running on hard surfaces when building up endurance

- Advising on the appropriateness of upper body strength work with bowlers in particular and knowing who to seek advice from.

- Developing core stability

- Advising on a suitable gym or health club

- Making contact with the "club" physiotherapist on behalf of injured players and staying in touch with both the player and the physiotherapist during the rehabilitation phase. Preferential rates have been negotiated

- Making contact with the "club" optometrist following in-house eye tests of players and the identification of potential problems. (See section on 'eyes' below.) Preferential rates have again been negotiated.

There's nothing earth shattering in this list – just practical, basic advice. The important thing is that the players, or at least some of the players, believe the items on the list are part of becoming a successful cricketer.

In some cases the above has been in conjunction with a programme to lose weight during the close season, where the coach can be a prime motivator. See "Lifestyle" section.

Simple advice can be found in *"Play Better Cricket"* in chapter 4 'Fitness Training', chapter 5 'Training Methods' and Appendix B 'The Principles of Training'. The ECB Level II course includes additional advice in part two of the supplementary information section 6 page 8.87. Advanced guidance in planning a programme and in more advanced training techniques are available to those coaches who reach the ECB Level III standard.

There is a lot in this area that a coach will find helpful if physical fitness is a high priority for a particular team. This book, however, isn't designed to provide the extensive knowledge required. Specialist courses and personal reading will be a more appropriate route. (See the comment at the end of this chapter after "Lifestyle".)

On the other hand, the following simple ideas will hopefully encourage the club coach to explore areas where they can make a difference.

- The eyes
- The skin
- The feet
- The muscles
- Dehydration
- Energy depletion.

Eyes

Presentations from "sports vision" specialists have convinced me that the eyes are the most neglected area of attention. I have always been aware that peripheral vision was important to cricket but have been forced to consider other important facts. Statements like: "Sight is what we see, vision is what we do with what we see, vision is trainable" and "You would have to walk 50,000 miles for your leg muscles to get the exercise that your eyes get in one day." It doesn't matter whether 50,000 is accurate, the point still gets across that the eyes are driven by muscles and that they are absolutely crucial to our performance and yet most of a team will rarely get them tested unless they have a known deficiency and probably almost none ever warm them up ready for use!

The ECB Level III course includes a section on "Sports Vision" and a "Visual Acuity Chart" is provided which includes instructions as to how to test eyesight. I've used it and discovered players who need a more formal assessment! It has also become routine practice to check on lens cleanliness with players who use contact lenses.

Although it may take time to convince players, I am encouraging them to warm up their eyes before competition and to top up that exercise if a batter is waiting to go into bat, etc. For example, during the pre-match warm-up I have taken a mini-bat which is used for catching practice and asked the players to focus first on the top of the handle and then at the splice and to jump between the two. (Another simple idea would be to use your hands and move them around and ask players to track each hand alternately.) This precedes game related practices involving a ball. Hopefully the message will get across.

I am also convinced that there is more for the top club coach to learn in relation to the training of the eyes to make them more efficient. Simon Falk and Simon Hollyhead wrote a very interesting article on "Vision Training in Cricket" that was published in the 1998 edition of the *Association of Cricket Coaches Journal*. (3) There isn't the space to go into detail now, but the article included several ideas as to how the eyes could be trained. The important thing for the coach to recognise is that a reduction in time between the stimulus and an accurate and controlled response (of batters and fielders in particular) is desirable and that this can be trained.

The other area I comment on is the choice of sunglasses. There are top quality sunglasses available, which prevent harmful rays entering the eyes and also reduce light intensity and improve contrast. Carefully chosen they can be very useful and important, but too many players frequently wear the wrong lens for the brightness of the sun or wear them for the wrong reason, and this on occasions, leads to 'dropped' catches when the object is to increase the chances of success. It is important to choose the right lens for the conditions and therefore interchangeable lenses are an advantage. It's better to learn techniques to avoid looking at the sun than to wear inappropriate lenses. The light enhancing lenses, however, are most impressive in dull conditions.

Skin

I am not an expert on skin, but the evidence is quite conclusive that exposure to the sun is becoming increasingly dangerous to our health in the United Kingdom. This has been long recognised in, for example, Australia where there is a culture of protection and widely promoted educational resources to encourage the young.

There appears to be universal agreement that the depletion of the ozone layer leaves us more vulnerable to the ultra violet rays of the sun that cause skin cancer. As coaches we therefore have a responsibility to the younger generation to encourage self-protection at all times.

Protection against skin cancer is not the only reason for advocating "30+ factor block" or "30+ factor Zinc sticks". (The latter for the nose and cheekbones, which are particularly susceptible to reflected glare.) Prolonged exposure to the sun when fielding can drain even the most motivated of performers. When combined with dehydration issues (see below) players recognise the importance and relationship of the two factors to the maintenance of concentration during the latter stages of a playing session.

Feet

When it comes to playing in a match, most players have thought about their footwear and make a conscious choice as to whether to wear full spikes, half spikes or rubbers. The coach in most circumstances will not get involved unless there is a problem with the feet of a particular player. There are, however, situations where it might be appropriate to pass comment. Some players for reasons of comfort wear rubbers when the playing conditions indicate that half or full spikes might be a better option. Examples are when the ground is wet, or when the grass is very green, or when the pitch is bare but the batter runs on an adjoining green strip. Wickets will be lost when batting and not taken when fielding because of poor choice of footwear! In the ideal world, players will have several pairs of boots: for bowling, fielding and batting, but in the end, cost and personal preference has to be considered.

The area where the coach can make more of a difference is when training or practice is indoors. Coaches should be aware of the absorption factor of different surfaces and recognise the massive difference between playing on concrete, on turf and on some of the more recent synthetic surfaces. Bowlers particularly need to be protected.

There are an enormous number of trainers on the market and frequently it is a case of "getting what you pay for". The choice can include running shoes, basketball boots/shoes, cross trainers and cricket rubbers.

Whatever is chosen the coach can have influence by recommending two things: cell technology for the cushioning effect and a policy of frequent renewal. The latter can be encouraged by suggesting that older trainers can move from the sporting arena to the social or casual arena and for this cycle to become repetitive in order to wear the newest possible for cricket.

Footwear and surfaces, as issues, get particular attention in the ECB Level III course.

Muscles

The reason for including muscles is that they often become sore. Soreness can arise during the latter stages of significant exercise, or its immediate aftermath, or at any time from 12-48 hours after heavy work, e.g., a long innings or bowling stint. The reason for soreness, be this inflammation or muscle damage, need not concern the coach unless they want to become a specialist in this area. Helping to prevent soreness however can be important.

The three things I encourage and expect are:

- That training should start with low intensity and gradually increase

- That warming up can reduce injury/damage/soreness

- That warming down helps reduce soreness especially when it is combined with stretching to increase flexibility.

The hardest of the three to develop as habit is the warm down.

Aspects of training are developed in both the ECB Level II "Sports Science" Supplement where improving strength is featured and in the ECB Level III course where special emphasis, amongst other things, is given to developing 'core/trunk stability' and 'stronger abdominals and back'.

A coach is always on the lookout for ways to motivate his/her team and keeping an open mind on new ideas can be helpful. One such 'new' way of body conditioning is "Pilates" which seems to have particular relevance to developing 'core stability'. The system promotes a method whereby it targets the deep postural muscles and builds strength from the inside out. Early attempts with one or two bowlers have proved very promising. The purpose of mentioning this is not to particularly promote the use of "Pilates" but to indicate that a coach who keeps an open mind will discover new motivational tools.

Another underestimated exercise that can be of great benefit is swimming. This is not the place to go into the physiological benefits of swimming, other than to say that the buoyancy that water gives the body reduces the internal pressure on the moving parts that are particularly connected with the movement of joints. It is also a great medium in which to perform stretches as the chances of injury are much reduced. Swimming can also be extremely beneficial in the rehabilitation phase after injury and as a "chill out" after a heavy physical workload.

Dehydration

It has already been mentioned in the paragraphs on skin above, that skin protection and dehydration when combined have a dramatic effect on concentration. I once read that water was second only in importance to oxygen and I've remembered it. I've also learned that it is possible to lose around 40% of body weight in fat, carbohydrate and protein and still survive but that this reduces to 9-12% of water before it can becomes life threatening, although I don't advocate trying this out!

The message is clear. Drinking fluids during prolonged exercise has important benefits especially during hot weather. Water can not only minimise dehydration but also reduce body temperature and cardio-vascular stress. Players need to be encouraged to drink plenty of water approximately one hour before performance and to top this up just prior to going on the field. If a player feels thirsty before taking on water, it is too late and performance will already have been affected. It is good practice to make drinks available to players, especially bowlers, throughout their time on the field in addition to the formal drinks breaks. Enlightened umpires will not prevent it unless it appears to be a time-wasting tactic.

The end of play is another important time for replenishing water levels especially if there is another game on the following day.

The ECB Level II course provides additional information in the Level II Manual "Sports Science" Supplement.

Energy depletion

Though less important than dehydration, energy sources can become depleted during a game and lead to a dip in performance. The ECB Level II course provides additional material in its "Sports Science" Manual Supplement, where advice is given on matchday diet amongst other things.

Essentially, coaches need to remind players to eat a high carbohydrate meal approximately 2-3 hours before performance and to top this up with convenient energy sources, such as bananas, just prior to the start of the game.

The players at Wolverhampton have time and time again seen the wisdom of this form of preparation. The sharpness in the field lasts so much longer in a playing session if energy sources and water reserves are not depleted.

MENTAL

This is an area, which was prioritised by Wolverhampton Cricket Club, as the side were young and inexperienced. The mental aspects can again be seen in the wagon wheel examples at the end of chapter two. They are taken from the *"Coach's Manual"*. They include concentration, motivation, awareness, practice ethic, enjoyment, consistency, toughness and confidence. Stephen Bull et al in their excellent book *"The Mental Game Plan"* add visualisation (imagery), anxiety control (arousal management), injury (recovery), group dynamics (team) and competitive preparation (professional).

I am not proposing to go through each of these mental qualities but to give examples of how some of them have become part of the work I have done with individual players and the team. *"The Mental Game Plan"* and *"Play Better Cricket"* are must-reads in this area. They are an invaluable resource for the club coach. For the less experienced coach, *"Play Better Cricket"* is perhaps the best starting point.

To establish a starting point in this area the individual player profiles (see chapter 4 for more details) pinpoint the areas that players think are important to them. In the reviews that led up to the 2000 season, the following mental areas for improvement were listed. They are in no particular order.

- Advice on reference books concerning the development of mental skills

- Develop mental toughness

- Cope better with selection policies

- Maintain confidence and get out of "dips" quickly

- Finding ways of avoiding putting the blame for "my" failure on events which are "out of my" control when the real cause is "within my control" (This is part of what is called "attribution" and affects both individual players and teams. See section on Team below)

- Handling expectation

- Dealing with "sledging"

- Preventing aggregates and averages from inhibiting the way I play

- Concentration

- Pre-match preparation

- How to keep things simple and avoid over complication

- Developing an approach which takes one ball at a time

- Develop the "killer" instinct in order to finish games off

- Cope better with disappointment

- Developing positive thinking

- Develop "recollections of quality performances"

- Develop "personal statements of affirmation" i.e. what I'm good at

- Develop consistency and control

Individual (one-to-one) coaching

The areas, which the players identify as needing the most attention, are the development of confidence, consistency, concentration and toughness. From a coaching point of view I would add awareness. For a young side, motivation, the practice ethic and enjoyment are generally part and parcel of their involvement.

When it comes to confidence, consistency and concentration I usually link them together and I always start with concentration. Quality concentration solves many apparent difficulties and before any other strategy is tried, I believe that concentration must be eliminated as a cause. This reappears as a theme in the section on the technical.

I am in no doubt that if concentration is where it should be, then the quality performer will achieve greater consistency. Greater consistency then leads to increased confidence. That's what I call keeping it simple, otherwise the coach is in danger of putting the cart before the horse and trying to correct a symptom and not a cause.

If concentration does not hit the jackpot (and it frequently does) then perhaps look for improvement elsewhere, but not until you have established what the player understands by concentration. The book "Play Better Cricket" has many good sections for the aspiring coach. Not least is the section on concentration, including concentration triggers, in chapter two. I come back to concentration a little later.

The above is the way I approach consistency and confidence via concentration, but there are also times when, for example, confidence has to be worked on as a separate issue. Recollections (or even video recordings) of past performances of quality can assist here in a major way, but I also think that the coach can subtly influence confidence by the way they talk about players. One specific technique to help build confidence in an individual player is to talk positively about the player's quality in front of another member of the team, or to deliberately make complimentary comments to someone else, in the knowledge that the player will overhear what is being said about them. Timing and situation are both important.

The players identified 18 areas for improvement in the list, but I don't propose to go into the details here of how I deal with their requested priorities. Some examples can be found in chapter 4 - "Communication".

It would be possible to work on mental training with a particular player and to almost follow a course, but that approach would be too heavy for many. If, however, the coach responds to a request as a result of a player review (see chapter 4), then the skill for the coach is to know where to look for the appropriate information to work on that specific area.

There are several ways to identify the most appropriate area to work on with a particular player. They can all help a player to pinpoint areas in need of attention. They can also assist in the definition of his/her goals and contribute to the creation of targets.

• The player can complete a "Mental Skills Questionnaire".

One such questionnaire can be found in *"The Mental Game Plan"* where the answers to questions indicate areas of strength and areas to work on. This questionnaire focuses on 7 mental skills - Imagery, Mental Preparation, Self-confidence, Anxiety and Worry, Concentration, Relaxation and Motivation.

This questionnaire would make a good starting point for a coach

• Another good starting point would be for the player to complete
   a performance profile. Again, this process can be found in
   "The Mental Game Plan". It essentially involves the player in
   describing the qualities they wish to acquire and then comparing
   their current skill level with their ideal skill level (ratings out of
   10). The bigger the discrepancy the more it suggests work is
   needed in that area.

• I have found that players sometimes find it difficult to identify
   qualities they want to acquire. One alternative method that I
   have used to overcome this is to focus on what makes a "winner".
   This approach looks at the end product and it often helps the
   performer to see the qualities required more easily. The following
   list gives a few examples. You may not agree with all of them.
   A full list can be found on the next page, although you will probably
   be able to make up your own if you find this approach useful.
   The way the list is used is to ask the players to read the list and
   to identify the qualities they would like to acquire. I am adding to

- Winners turn difficult situations into opportunities
- Winners see difficult situations as opportunities to excel
- Winners believe adversity brings out their best talents
- Winners see challenges not threats
- Winners enjoy the process of solving problems
- Winners avoid forcing situations
- Winners see the value of mental techniques
- Winners use averages and aggregates to motivate rather than inhibit
- Winners avoid looking too far ahead and stay focused in the present
- Winners know the value of routine: pre-match
- Winners know the value of routine: pre-innings, pre-bowling/fielding/wicket keeping
- Winners regularly review progress
- Winners have a good attitude achieved through habit and desire
- Winners avoid putting pressure on themselves by "Just doing their best"
- Winners appear to effortlessly succeed and frequently camouflage their hard work.
- Winners are comfortable with themselves
- Winners recognise the value of visualisation
- Winners are caught less by surprise
- Winners recognise the value of self-talk
- Winners get out of "dips in performance" quicker
- Winners exhibit intensity yet remain calm
- Winners recognise that anxiety is what a player is thinking
- Winners realise that anger disrupts
- Winners control their nerves and have lower anxiety
- Winners can find the space to smile amid the challenge
- Winners seek better ways
- Winners attend practice
- Winners listen to colleagues
- Winners avoid 'closed' thinking to change
- Winners avoid negative language and criticism of colleagues
- Winners know that every ball is an event
- Winners support their teammates through thick and thin
- Winners enjoy partnerships with teammates – batting and bowling
- Winners make the most of every practice opportunity
- Winners enjoy both practice and matches
- Winners socialise more after matches
- Winners realise that a match is the culmination of a process.

my own list of "What makes a winner" all the time.

The above three methods can be used in a players review. Different players respond to different methods, so the coach must remain flexible in approach. If the outcome resulted in a request for a strategy to be developed, I would like to think that I would be able to give constructive advice and support. The coach can't be expected to know everything however, and even experienced coaches often need to research. The important thing for the coach is that he/she knows where to look for support information.

Working on "Concentration" as an example

There is a vast area of work in the above areas that a coach can do with members of a team. The **bold** "winners" in the next list all relate to concentration and I make this an example. The assumed situation is that the player has indicated that he/she wants to work on "concentration", or has been helped to recognise that it is an area that would benefit from development via any of the three methods described above. The coach could then use the list of statements in bold as coat pegs on which to communicate his/her response to the player if appropriate.

The work with the player will be fairly simple to start with and will revolve around the word "routine". The routines I have tried to establish and which have had some success are based on three triggers - the first visual, the second physical and the third verbal - or *see* something, *do* something, *say* something. For example, a bowler will consciously switch off and relax following a delivery, decide what he/she is going to bowl next on the way back to the beginning of their run and then switch on and go through a set routine. The way I communicate the "routine" is developed in chapter 4.

The essential thing is that the bowler *looks* for a visual trigger from either the batter or the wicket keeper in their pre-delivery routine. This is followed by a routine of *doing* something with the ball such as spinning the ball "x" number of times from hand to hand or placing the fingers quite deliberately on the seam. And finally, *saying* something like "flow towards target" follows this. The exact detail of the triggers should be chosen by the player concerned, with every encouragement for them to develop something unique to themselves. The main thing is that the player should make this a unique routine and do it for every ball - routine, routine, routine.

The example given is for a bowler, but batters, fielders and wicket keepers should also be encouraged to use the same *see, do* and *say* concentration triggers.

Further examples of what makes a "Winner"

- Winners plan ahead

- Winners make their own luck

- Winners enjoy the battle of competition

- Winners respond well to adversity

- Winners produce their best when it matters

- Winners are mentally tough

- Winners give 100% all of the time

- Winners try to win every ball and regard each ball as an event

- Winners recognise that the next ball could change the game

- Winners win the contest with themselves

- Winners don't panic

- Winners see the value of a mental game plan

- Winners are well motivated

- Winners set goals and targets

- Winners know the value of routine

- Winners use past performance to maintain and develop their confidence

- Winners are positive and optimistic

- Winners cope well with expectation

- Winners have self-discipline, self-control and self-confidence

- Winners realise their potential

- Winners see the value of "what if" planning

- Winners develop 'personal statements of affirmation' - what they are good at

- Winners avoid looking back other than to learn

- Winners "bin" mistakes ("Look back & review - learn - 'bin' - look ahead")

- **Winners focus on the here and now, this moment, the next ball**

- **Winners know what relaxed concentration means**

- **Winners know what the "zone of concentration" means and enter it more often**

- **Winners concentrate better**

- **Winners are less easily distracted**

- Winners keep it simple and perform to their best

- Winners control their emotions especially anger and aggression
- Winners accept responsibility for their own performance
- Winners avoid blaming others
- Winners are always improving
- Winners practice more
- Winners work harder
- Winners listen to advice
- Winners are open to discussion
- Winners are consistent
- Winners think, "team"
- Winners think "my role" and "my contribution" to the whole team effort
- Winners finish the job off
- Winners treat the opposition with dignity and respect.

There is nothing earth shattering about what has just been written, and the example of "concentration triggers" just happens to be the one I've chosen because I think it is one of the most important ingredients in success.

My approach is to develop small modules or units of work (e.g., "concentration triggers") that I can use with individual players. Over time the range of prepared units cover an increasing area of mental skill development. It is important that the top coach has an understanding of a range of mental skill topics, while greater in-depth understanding involving more advanced techniques can then strengthen this breadth over time.

I repeat what I have said earlier that this book isn't designed to provide the extensive knowledge required. Specialist courses or personal reading starting with the books already mentioned, provide a rich source of information for the coach to feed on and will uncover a treasure trove of ideas. There are many other books for those who want to develop their expertise in the coaching of mental skills to their players.

Identifying the areas of need is one thing but communicating how to handle them is another. The requirement here is that knowledge and communication skills must go hand in hand. Together they play perhaps the central role in a successful coach. Some coaches will have knowledge but may be short of communication skills, while others have the communication skills and lack knowledge. The top coach has both and is ever striving to improve in both areas.

Team (Coaching)

If concentration triggers are part of each players preparation then this can be used when motivating the whole team or motivating units within the team, e.g., the seam bowlers, the spin attack, all the bowlers, the top 5 batters, the "boiler house" batters at 6-8, etc. It will often depend on the game situation, but some situations will be repetitive within a game and can be prepared for beforehand by the coach.

For example, a pre-match preparation might be what you say to the two opening bats and the number 3, suggesting being on the lookout to preserve their partner's concentration levels. Similarly, bowlers who work in pairs can also be encouraged to help their partner in the desire for both to retain concentration.

From a team point of view, the coach should be able to assume that the players know how to concentrate, based on one-to-one work that the coach has carried out previously. The next task is then to focus the whole team by using communication techniques to pull them together into a collective outfit that knows what it is trying to achieve. There is more on the communication methods used by the coach with the whole team in chapter 4. There are also some examples of team goals setting in chapter 5.

In the same way as I used concentration as an example in one-to-one coaching, I use team concentration as the example for team coaching and take one specific situation.

Working on concentration when the weather is poor

The weather is one factor that can have a highly significant effect on the approach of a team to a game. In match situations when rain is in the air, the levels of focus and concentration are often below where they need to be. The coach in these situations needs to be the researcher of local weather as journeys of 50-60 miles can make major differences. It's the weather where the team are at a particular time that matters to the psychology of the team. Knowing the correct Ceefax and Teletext numbers can prove very useful, not only on the day of the match but on the build up for several days beforehand. It becomes part of the coach's focus. The coach needs to focus well ahead if the timing with the preparation of the players is going to be "spot on".

For example, if it's raining in Wolverhampton and we have to travel 50 miles to an away venue, there is a risk that focus will be lost. The coach needs to have researched the local weather and know that the weather is, say, clearing from the south and that the venue for the day should be clear of rain at a much earlier time in the day (bad weather may not be even forecast at the destination ground). Whatever your research concludes, this needs to be communicated to the team if they are not to arrive expecting a washout. How I communicate this to players and do everything possible to keep their brains where they need to be can be found in the chapter 4 on communication.

An indicator of the mental state of players is in the time they arrive when rain is in the air, in relation to their normal timekeeping.

Tell tale signs are:

• Arriving late

• Body language as they arrive: is it a swagger, a stroll or a walk of purpose in comparison to normal?

• Coming into the dressing room without their coffin or kit bag

• The choice of conversation: Is it cricket based, about the weather, or is it a negative use of language in general.

Good observation of the above can indicate the task that the coach needs to address.

More general "Team" mental qualities and skills

Other aspects of what is required of the collective team mental effort is really bound up with communication and is dealt with in the chapters on preparation, communication and match action, but the essential qualities required of the team will frequently be the same or similar. What makes the difference is how the coach keeps them fresh in the way he/she deals with the team as a whole.

Some mental areas that might be pinpointed for the team include:

• Patience

• Determination

• Self-control

• Self-belief

• Bottle.

These were the mental qualities used in the successful ECB National Club Championship run in 1999 (see chapter 5 "Match Action").

Examples of others that I have used depending on circumstance include:

• Enjoyment

• Mental preparation

• Controlling the controllable

• Positive thinking

- Concentration

- Application

- Commitment

- Toughness

- Responsibility

- Partnerships

- Focus

- Respect for opposition

- Sowing seeds of doubt within the opposition (e.g., our top class fielding)

- Bouncing back.

The list can quite easily grow, as new ideas for motivating the team are uncovered. Each of the above can be used as a "coat peg", or a combination of "coat pegs", upon which to hang the motivating team talk prior to the start of a match (see team talks in chapter 4).

I use the same process to generate ideas for the team as I do with individuals by listing what makes a "winning" team. The list that follows applies to most of the list for individual "winners". A few examples are quoted:

- Winning teams plan ahead

- Winning teams make their own luck

- Winning teams enjoy the battle of competition

- Winning teams respond to adversity (adding "They are never beaten and fight to the very last ball)

- Winning teams are mentally tough

- Winning teams give 100% all of the time

- Winning teams don't panic

- Winning teams try to win every ball

- Winning teams have self-discipline, self-control and self-confidence

- Winning teams maintain their concentration

- Winning teams have strategies that define the role of each player

- Winning teams are consistent

- Winning teams control the controllable

- Winning teams enjoy both practice and matches

- Winning teams finish the job off.

The list could go on and on, but there is no need. Following the one-to-one coaching list and replacing "Winners" with "Winning teams" should provide plenty more "coat pegs" upon which to develop an approach to team mental preparation (see the "What Makes a Winner" list earlier in this chapter).

My approach to team mental skill development is similar to that used with individuals. It is to develop small modules or units of work (e.g., "controlling the controllable") that I can use when it is appropriate. It is possible to list the factors which are uncontrollable, and this can have the desired effect. A fuller explanation of what controlling the controllable means can be helpful in the right situation. Chapter 5 illustrates how I used the list approach in match 8 in the 2000 season when my antennae were telling me that blame was being laid in areas that were uncontrollable. There is more about "team attribution" or the reasons that are given to explain successful and unsuccessful performance in chapter 4 in the section on team communication where the example used is "controlling the controllable".

This aspect receives attention in the ECB Level III course where "attribution" is covered in some detail. This may sound theoretical, and certainly needs careful handling, if it's not to come over as a lecture!

The same applies to team preparation as to individual preparation – knowledge and communication must go hand in hand.

Specific considerations

In addition to working with individuals and teams as described, there are a number of specific situations that the top club coach may need to consider. They include:

- Working with the captain
- Working with the overseas player or professional
- Working with the all-rounder
- Working with senior players
- Working with "difficult" cricketers
- Working with injured players

To be successful with players, the coach needs to get to know the person as well as the cricketer. The difference between working with most players and working with the six categories above is that knowing the person and the player is even more important in these relationships. Chapter 4 deals with coach/player relationships in more detail.

Working with the captain

It is absolutely vital that the captain and coach have a good working relationship. There will be times when you don't agree, and in such circumstances the coach has no alternative but to back his captain in the public arena and especially in front of the team. The time to try and sort out difficulties and disagreements must surely be in the preparation before and the review after matches.

The coach does a lot of one-to-one work with players and it is important that the captain is kept informed of any ongoing areas being developed in order that the captain can support, and reinforce where appropriate, the improvements being attempted (see chapter 4 for more information about communication between the coach and the captain).

While the major skills involved for the coach are in communication, it should not be forgotten that captaincy also involves concentration, consistency and confidence amongst a whole armoury of other mental attributes and one-to-one work may be needed in just the same way as for a batter, bowler, fielder or wicket keeper. Captaincy is a tough job especially when things are going wrong.

The ECB Level III course covers captaincy and includes many insights, which help the coach to reflect on the needs of the captain and to recognise that the mental qualities required of a captain, which are vital to team success, are developed and not overlooked.

In my opinion, the ideal supportive structure is for the captain, vice captain and coach to work as a group of three, and for there to be regular planning and review meetings to monitor progress. An influential "senior pro" might also be invited to contribute on a regular or occasional basis (see working with senior players below).

Working with the overseas player or professional

The overseas player is frequently a role model within the club and this adds extra responsibility to an already "high expectation" situation. That is why I think it important to find extra one-to-one time for discussion.

There is a strong possibility that the overseas player/professional will have a coaching commitment as part of the contract, so investment in a relationship is worth the effort.

There are no secrets here, but email contact for example prior to them arriving in the country is one invaluable device, but it is equally important that you check out the living accommodation arrangements. If a player isn't comfortable in this area it can cause problems, which can sometimes enter the playing arena.

There may be many mental skill areas that a coach can work on with the overseas player/professional, but the above recognises the role that the player performs and recognises that personal security is an important issue for everyone especially someone from another country. My advice is "go the extra mile" - it pays dividends.

Working with senior players

Consideration and respect are words that can be overlooked in the competitive environment of a team game. If the coach expresses both towards senior players and tries to find ways of involving them, this can have a very beneficial effect on the mental edge they bring to the team.

Working with the all-rounder

The task of an all-rounder can be very demanding, and the coach needs to recognise that the mental qualities needed by the player and the support that is appropriate from the coach is not simply the addition of the support of a batter plus the support of a bowler. An all-rounder has a very special role, and can mentally have a massive psychological effect of the opposition. It is vital however that the all-rounder is mentally sound in both disciplines at the same time. A weakness in one can have a detrimental effect upon the other. The coach can have a significant effect on the mental psyche of the all-rounder.

Working with "difficult" players

If the coach knows his/her players as people as well as cricketers, then they have a head start. There are no easy solutions to difficult players, only a belief that time and effort has to be put into getting to know their ways. It is frequently the coach who can make a break through and this usually around the fact that the trouble was taken. It's again about "going the extra mile". The coach should not underestimate the effect he/she can have on the mental approach of a "difficult" player

Working with injured players

No one likes to get injured, but it's all too easy to forget players when it happens. The message is simple. If the coach wants to make sure that the player has the appropriate mental attitude when they return, then they must look after their needs while they are injured. Helping to arrange appropriate treatment is important.

Wolverhampton has an arrangement with a local physiotherapist who charges a beneficial club rate. He is also approachable and recognises that by working with the coach, he can have a significant effect on the mental well being of the player. It is also important to keep the player involved in practice (e.g., feeding the bowling machine) and in matches (helping and talking with the coach). All of this contributes to keeping them positive about their future playing prospects.

This section has been about the mental ingredient although some of the above points, and in other parts of the section, relate to communication. That is unavoidable because the two are inextricably linked. Developing the mental skills of players and managing their mental frame of mind are inseparable.

TECHNICAL

The coach is obviously expected to have an in-depth technical understanding of the game, but in top club cricket the main agenda item during a season will not be alteration of technique, but tactical and effective use of the technique that players already possess.

The more advanced a coach becomes, the more likely he/she is to be working with players who have developed distinctive personal habits. Coaching will therefore focus less on *how* a skill is performed and more on *why* and *when* a particular skill is deployed. It's about making quality judgements and recognising the overlap of the technical and tactical.

The main time to work on or alter technique is in the off-season after the end of season rest. In practical terms this is likely to be from about January onwards for the top club player and will inevitably have to be indoors. During the season however, it is still possible to introduce new skills on the understanding that this is a developmental exercise, although a club season usually presents opportunities in non-league games when new skills can be attempted. Implementation of new skills in a top league game should only be attempted when the skill has been conquered to a reasonably high standard. Carefully handled, the introduction of new skills can help motivation.

Only if a player is in serious trouble and going through a major crisis would I consider significant technical intervention during the season. I would try other strategies first rather than risk making things worse by inappropriate intervention. Reference is made at the end of this section to the importance of concentration, but working on confidence can also be valuable. Asking a player to recollect their "top ten performances" or refer to their list of "what they are good at" can make a significant difference to the player. It can be a tough call as to which approach to employ.

In the end, the coach's response needs to be tailored to fit the individual player, and for some, discussions about technique and/or reminders of successful changes that have been made in the past are appropriate. There is no substitute for "knowing your players". Your judgement as to whether to intervene technical or to leave alone could prove vital in a season. Choose wisely and it could make a season take off for a player, choose poorly and you could cause greater confusion. The quality coach makes the correct decisions more often!

What a coach can do in the season is recognise quality performance when it is exhibited and, where appropriate, follow this up with a comment that reinforces the technical reason for the successful execution of a particular skill. This helps reinforce good habits and builds confidence and is a vital part of the communication with players that is developed in chapter 4.

The exception to avoiding or reducing technical intervention is probably fielding where I believe it is possible to be making technical improvements all the time. This is partly because the skill threshold of fielding is more manageable and partly because the opportunity to develop this dimension of the game is limited during the winter. Fielding practice and development is in any case a vital aspect of team morale and team success.

The ECB Coaching Scheme covers technique in depth and the accompanying "Coach's Manual" is quite superb. In terms of cricket technique, the Level I course introduces 16 skills: 7 batting, 4 bowling, 4 fielding and 1 wicket keeping. The Level II course then follows this up with a further 11 batting, 8 bowling and 3 fielding skills. The Level III course looks at technique in more detail and relates it to the other "vital ingredients". Wicket keeping also receives much more attention, while batting becomes divided into batting against pace or spin, and bowling into its specialist categories. Fielding also gets divided in specialist infield, outfield and close catching.

The Level II course introduces coaches to the analysis of performance and includes performance profiling (see "Wagon Wheels" at the end of chapter two) and the very valuable tool of video analysis. The Level II course concentrates on the video analysis of batting and bowling, while the Level III course introduces the video analysis of fielding and wicket keeping and extends the batting and bowling analysis to include tactical awareness as well as technical skill. Carefully used, it can be a very potent resource because it can provide evidence of what players do well, as well as indicate areas for improvement.

The Level II course introduces the fundamentals of quality coaching and describes and reinforces them in the sequential analytic process of:

➤ *Observation*   ➤ *Analysis*   ➤ *Evaluation*

➤ *Feedback*   ➤ *Planning*   ➤ *Further Observation etc.*

Coaches need a consistent method of analysis if they are to be successful and the Level II course helps significantly to develop this skill.

The Level II course also introduces the important concept of how we learn new skills using the analogy of learning to drive a car. Paraphrased it includes 4 stages:

1. When a new skill is attempted, many mistakes are made, but the performer doesn't recognise they are making them.

2. Mistakes are still made but the performer is aware that they are mistakes.

3. The performer is aware that they are performing the skills correctly.

4. The performer performs the skills correctly but they have become automatic.

At top club level, coaches mainly deal with stages 2, 3 and 4, but it's when the majority of skills are being performed, in technical terms, to level 4, that the coach is most likely to make the progress with how mental and tactical dimensions can be added.

Technique at the higher levels of club cricket will focus more on adapting to specific situations and using knowledge of technique to affect the outcome of a phase of play during a match. For example, the coach can develop specific strategies for playing on different surfaces. Once the techniques have been developed for a particular surface, then they can be integrated into a tactical approach to a match situation. The two go hand in glove; using the appropriate technique is a pre-requisite of correct tactical implementation.

Playing on early season wickets

This is taken as an example of how a coach can help players to adapt their technique. At this stage it isn't in a match context and is therefore technical. When the same skills are applied to a simulated match situation in practice, or in a match, it becomes tactical.

Technically one of the most common "ways of thinking" that a club coach will be trying to communicate to players in the early season is how to bat and bowl on wet, slow and low pitches.

For batting on wet, slow and low pitches I coach playing the ball late. I talk of a large dustbin lid which is the size of a "wheelie bin" and of letting the ball come into the batters space within this dustbin lid and not letting the wrists move outside it. In other words the batter is in control if the ball enters his/her large dustbin lid and lost control if the hands make contact with the ball outside it. Add to this the softness with which the ball leaves the bat and you have a basic formula or strategy for a particular set of conditions. This can lead to greater security and the preservation of a batters wicket and increases the chances of manipulating the ball in order to keep the scoreboard ticking over with singles. Alternatively if you decide to strike the ball firmly when the ball is outside the "wheelie bin lid zone", then there can be no half measures. The power of the shot must go through the ball and send it well over the top.

For bowlers it is using the same technical information to influence the selection of what delivery to bowl. In this case, the bowlers will be trying to get the batter to push their hands outside their "wheelie bin" zone and into the area of "loss of control" which implies pitching the ball up. There may be the need in some cases to give pointers as to how to pitch the ball up, but in general that won't be necessary with the quality performer.

The emphasis is not so much on changing technique but applying existing skills with more care and thought. The above example was for playing on early season wickets, but the principle could be applied to numerous situations, for example, turning wickets, flat tracks, bouncy tracks etc.

Batting, bowling and fielding drills

There is a place for practising outside a conventional net situation and to perform "drills" in isolation. If a **batter** is able to sweep for example, conventional net practice provides limited opportunities. The setting up of a drill whereby the sweep can be played 30 or 40 times consecutively will undoubtedly improve its execution and thereby make it more likely to succeed in a match. In a carefully constructed practice, it would be possible for player "a" to look at the last part of the shot and to start in almost the end position (on one knee), in order to isolate the precise technical aspects at the point of impact and then move backwards until the stroke is generated from the stance position. For player "b" it might be appropriate to start from the stance position. Part of the practice will be refining technique but it will also be reinforcing correct technique and providing the basis of confidence to use the technique in a game. The sweep is one example for which a drill can be constructed with the aid of either a bowling machine or a hand fed service.

It would be just as easy to set up drills to reinforce correct techniques in other situations. The following examples particularly emphasise decision making:

- **"Deciding whether to play, duck or sway against the fast bouncing ball".**
  This can be a paired activity whereby tennis balls are delivered under-arm towards the batter who decides whether to play, duck or sway. This can then be extended by the use of a tennis ball wrapped

in insulating tape which can be thrown down to simulate a bouncing ball. This type of ball is much less hard than a cricket ball but provides similar rebound characteristics.

- **"Strategies against the swinging ball".**
  This can again be a paired activity where masking tape, or similar, is wrapped round half of a tennis ball. If the tennis ball is gripped with the orthodox grip for outswing or inswing as if the shiny side was the tennis ball side and the rough side the taped side, then the ball swings significantly. This service from a partner enabled strategies to be devised for each batter. A bowling machine can also be set up to produce a swinging effect.

- **"Manipulating the field against spinners".**
  A practice can be set up to simulate a spin bowlers flight and for the batter to make decisions concerning identical deliveries as to whether to move out of the crease to play with a straight bat or to sweep from the crease. This skill can then be applied tactically as a strategy against accurate quality bowling. Again a bowling machine can also be used.

- **"Moving out to drive, hit over the top or defend".**
  A decision making practice that views moving out of the crease as a "basis for a negotiation", not a commitment. This can then be applied tactically as a way to break down a spinners field and can be used in association with "Manipulating the field".

- **Practices, which focus on the "collision speed" of the ball onto the bat.**
  The batter is encouraged to use different collision speeds of bat on ball and to notice the changes that take place in where the ball finishes up. This can then be used tactically to show how "singles can be pinched" or how "2's can be constructed in place of hard hit 1's". Cones can be placed at different distances from the batter and the batter has to say which cone is the target.

- **Practices, which develop front foot defensive play against the turning ball.**
  For example, right handed batter using the front pad on the line that the ball is following, with the bat alongside the pad in anticipation of the leg spin deviation, or, for the off spinning ball, using the bat on the line that the ball is following and the front leg alongside in anticipation of the turn but "covering" the possible straight ball. This sort of practice would be attended by advice about the limitations of such a method but would give a strategy for the player having difficulty. This practice could also be converted into attack using the same principles.

- **Practices, which develop the correct technique when running between the wickets.**
  This includes carrying the bat, turning with a low centre of gravity and using the arm as an extension of the bat handle and the curved edge of the bat to avoid friction between bat and ground. This sort of practice can be performed over the length of a pitch or with reduced dimensions, even perhaps within a rectangle with arrows indicating the next direction to take. This practice, especially the latter rectangular version, can also be a very good fitness exercise.

Other drills could be devised to improve footwork, or for that matter any other aspect or skill. The limitations are only the limits of the imagination. The main difference when coaching at top club level is that while the technical position of head, hands and feet are still very important, the coach is more concerned with balance, weight transfer and control. In the end it is about the effectiveness, even if there is some unorthodoxy, of the decision making process and the quality of the judgements that are made. The ECB Level III course provides considerable detail in this area and numerous examples of drills, which could be employed. The imagination of the coach is the other resource!

Bowlers could also be provided with drills to reinforce correct technique without the extra complication of the batter. The skills are simpler to devise than for a batter as the bowler generates the skill ("closed skill"), whereas the batter makes a response to a perception of the ball in flight ("open skill").

Examples include:

- Seam bowlers bowling down the "corridor of uncertainty" with string/cord indicating the corridor.

- Bowlers "following through straighter", again by using string/cord to indicate the line. This helps to reduce/avoid the bowler pulling away with the front arm and shoulder.

- Bowlers bowling "close to the stumps" by narrowing the channel through which to run up and particularly deliver the ball.

- Swing bowlers using "Bowling accuracy monitoring charts" to track intention and outcome (see end of chapter two).

- Spin bowlers bowling at "mat targets or cone targets" for right and left hand batters. The cones are particularly good to indicate the corridor while the mats are better for providing a target.

- Spin bowlers using real or artificial "worn" areas in which to bowl. Cutting a target from an old indoor mat and then turning it over, honeycomb up, could construct the artificial situation.

- Bowlers practising "caught and bowled" by bowling a ball and the coach hitting a tennis ball with a tennis racket straight back at them after the appropriate time delay.

- Bowlers practising "stopping a single" and "run outs" by bowling a ball and the coach rolling a slow moving ball to one side or the other of a line between the wickets.

As with batting, the main difference when coaching bowling at top club level is that while technique is still important, the coach is more concerned with the bowler understanding their own action and with their recognition of the qualities required to be consistent. This varies, depending on the type of bowler, and might include such things as self-awareness of their particular run up, grip, position of the wrist in delivery and follow through. Provided the action is safe in the case of pace bowlers, it's about the effectiveness, even if there is some unorthodoxy, of the decision making process. It's also about the quality of the judgements that are made in determining what to bowl to which type of batter in which match situation. The ECB Level III course develops this line of thought and co-ordinates an appreciation of the combined effect of the technical with the tactical, mental and physical.

Fielding lends itself to drills and is extremely valuable in the development of team spirit. It can be made great fun. I'm not proposing to give many examples here as there is source information available. The drills below are examples:

- Practice to learn how to catch when the ball is coming out of the sun, by rotating the body position to place a different background from the sun into view.

- Practice to encourage improvisation when "catching on the move" when normal technique isn't possible.

- Simulating bat/pad catching with the ball rebounding off a soft object

- Distraction catching where groups of 4-8 players, each with a ball, throw to their partner across the face of the clock. Each pair stands opposite each other at, for example, quarter past and quarter to the hour, etc.

- Creating a practice environment (a deliberately over watered area of unimportant grass) in which players in very old clothes can develop the skill of the sliding pick up and throw.

- Developing specialist-fielding positions by targeting practice for specific players rather than generalised practice for everyone.

Two useful sources for ideas are: "The Complete Book of Modern Fielding Practices" by Chris Stone (4) and the "Tacklesport" CD Rom (5) called "Animated Skill Drills for Cricket Coaching".

Wicket keeping also lends itself to drills, although there is less source information available for ideas. The ideas are generally carried around in the heads of skilled practitioners! A few examples would include:

- Working in pairs and catching with preferred hand and non-preferred hand.
- Catching the half volley
- Practice which aids concentration by having to name the colour of a ball being thrown towards the keeper.
- Catching, standing back, when the ball is thrown onto a ridged surface (upturned shower matting or similar). The ball deviates laterally but is unpredictable.
- Practising running up to the wicket to collect a throw-in.
- Diving practice - good fun if a "crash mat" is available.

In many cases, the fielding and wicket keeping practices are inter-changeable. The ECB Level III course develops close catching, "on the 1" in fielding, "fielding in the deep" out fielding and wicket keeping in much more depth.

By taking these skills out of context, the player is able to focus on the technique. The examples offered are merely a small sample of what could be devised. Carefully used, this has a place although it is undoubt-edly applied skill to tactical situations, which is the real objective and brings the drills to life.

Final thought in this section

It was stated earlier that I am prepared to engage in the technical coaching of players during the season on a one-to-one basis if it feels right for a particular player. The coaching, however, will be of broad technical importance and avoid too much detail.

If a player comes to me with what is called a technical problem, my first reaction is to suggest that it could well be concentration. So although concentration is a mental quality, it often impinges on the technical aspect of a player's game. Only when concentration has been eliminated as the cause of the perceived deficiency am I prepared to look further. Time and time again a player has said something like "I want you to look at my bowling action, I'm spraying the ball down the leg side too often " or something like "I want you to look at where I'm picking up my bat, I think it's going to gully and causing me to hit across the line", and time and time again, dealing with concentration and about the desired end product has solved the perceived problem without technique being mentioned once. This isn't always the case but I would advise starting with concentration.

TACTICAL

You can "read all about it" and "talk all about it", but in the end a tactical analysis of what took place in a game is vital if experience is going to lead to future improvement. Some of the analysis can be carried out in a post-match debrief but specific tactical development in many cases needs to be tackled through one-to-one discussion. This is particularly important if game-by-game benefits are going to be maximised for young players.

Players can often identify, or contribute to the identification of their own needs when it comes to physical, mental, technical and lifestyle issues even if they can only provide some of the answers. The tactical area is different because it deals with what players don't know about playing the game. This is what makes it so important at top club level and why it matters that the coach has a strategy to cover this essential area. It doesn't mean that players are unable to interpret what is happening in a game, it just means that more guidance is needed from the coach. While a lot of tactical awareness can be developed from how the coach's side play, the tactics used by the opposition are sometimes more difficult to identify.

The tactical area is not something that can be coached in isolation.

It's about the coach, and where appropriate captain, vice-captain and senior players:

- Taking opportunities to explain what is going on in a game to the players
- Identifying "magic moments" in which a game can or does change shape
- Identifying quality decisions that were made in the interests of the team
- Identifying selfishness where it resides
- Identifying and exploiting strength within the team
- Identifying and exploiting weakness in the opposition
- Encouraging all players to think like a captain

An example of how the coach can make a difference is to look at pre-season preparation. This is particularly important with a talented, young but inexperienced side. You can't put experience where it hasn't been, so the coach has the job of either simulating game situations or constructing match practice to get within touching distance of what will be required.

I believe that indoor net practice can make an important contribution. First of all, at top club level, we need to rid ourselves of the 'social slog' mentality that often accompanies pre-season preparation. I certainly won't offer my service if that is what the players think is appropriate. It might be right for some clubs but not for clubs who want to succeed, to win things, or to gain promotion and to enjoy the satisfaction that goes with quality performance.

The coach can create a realistic practice if he/she defines a game situation and asks the batter and bowlers to perform appropriately. This might be with one batter, or with two batters in a "Running Net" as described in chapter 2 in the section called "A Typical Practice Session". It helps if the coach explains the field settings, so shot selection and bowling can be tailored more precisely. This can be not only a positive learning experience of the "what if" kind but also good fun. And it can be extended to a paired "Dismissed Net" situation where the batters change places if the batter is dismissed.

The following are examples of skills that top club players should either know or be learning.

Batters:
- Rotating the strike - especially the left handed/right handed combination, with the implied emphasis on picking up singles.

- Exploiting the inner ring in order to score singles, which implies observation by both batters of the position fielders have adopted, and agreement as to their concentration level (or lack of it) and mobility (or lack of it).

- Exploiting the outer ring in order to make 1's into 2's. This implies equally astute observation, not only of field placement but also of the sprinting speed and throwing arm of a particular fielder. It also demands an understanding on the part of the striker as to the force of the ball off the bat. (See technique section)

- Who is best placed to face which bowler in which situation. This sometimes means the established batter giving the strike to the forceful newly arrived batter. Alternatively, in difficult situations, one batter faces one bowler and the other batter faces the other. The decision usually rests on what is the easier ball to play and that is most often the ball coming into the batter.

- Sacrificing a wicket and being "run out" in order to keep the "right" batter at the wicket. (Especially during run chases.)

- Manipulating or dismantling the field in order to force field changes open up other scoring angles and opportunities.

down the wicket to spin bowlers on a difficult wicket in to take close catchers out of play.

atters "getting out of the traps" - looking for quick singles

Bowlers:

- Seam bowlers bowling to a plan, to which a field can be set, of targeting the "corridor of uncertainty" on an off stump and just outside off stump line.

- Seam bowlers using round the wicket as a variation for right-handed batters and maybe as a strategy for left-handed batters. This tests the ability of the batter to know where the off stump is from two different lines of attack. Batters are not always equally good at the decision making involved.

- Bowlers, especially spin bowlers, probing the "San Andreas" fault, i.e., finding out where the threshold is between a batter playing the ball to leg or off and then exploiting that line. This will vary from batter to batter.

- Spin bowlers using over and round the wicket deliveries to either exploit the rough or create a different challenge for the batter

- Strategies for making it difficult for the batter when attacking, at the end of an innings or during a one day knock out match especially at the death:

    - Bowling full and straight rather than short and wide

    - Bowling at a "plant pot" between the batters legs in stance position

    - Bowling to hit the back leg shin in a batters stance.

All three methods deny the batter leverage with no arcs available for striking through the ball.

- Counteracting the "charge" of a batter by following the batter and aiming at the legs

- Bowlers identifying faults in a batter and then exploiting them.

Fielders:

- Fielders identifying faults and anticipating the likely outcome of batters shot selection

- Interpreting body language and "sniffing" that batters are after quick singles, and timing the surge when walking in towards the batter to sow doubt in the batters mind.

- Observing eye contact between batters and body language in general to indicate what they are thinking, e.g., looking or nodding towards space, playing shadow shots, etc.

- Recognising that shuttle throwing is on occasions more likely to achieve a run out than one long throw. The shuttle gives the middle player the option of which end to throw at.

- Inner ring fielders giving false clues to the batting side, e.g., cover stands square to the wicket but sometimes walks in at an angle towards the bowler or the middle of the pitch rather than directly towards the batter, and hence makes the decision making of the batters more difficult. This can and does create run out opportunities when well executed.

- Inner ring fielders walking in at different speeds so that the batters have more difficulty in predicting where they will be at the point of impact on the bat. This is best used alongside anticipation as to whether the batter is going to play a defensive or attacking shot. The best fielders have an instinct for when a defensive or attacking shot is going to be played because they have the ability to "see inside the batters head" and know what is being thought.

- Fielders "on the two" in the outfield taking into account the position of the pitch when it is not central and moving in 5-10 metres to ensure that a two isn't offered on a plate.

- Close catches, e.g., slip fielders adjusting their position according to the batting style. This implies astute assessment of a batters technique.

Team:
- Being aware of the dimensions and angles of a playing arena, particularly in unorthodox grounds, and protecting the short vulnerable boundaries.

- Being aware of wind direction and its likely influence. Examples include, with the description used relevant to right-handed batters:

    - If the wind is coming from third man, it will benefit the right arm over and left arm over inswing bowlers (the latter is outswing to a left-handed batter).

    - If the wind is coming from fine leg, it will benefit the off spin bowler especially when the "floater" is attempted. This wind will also help the right arm and left arm outswing bowler (the latter is inswing to a left-handed batter).

    - If the wind is coming in over mid on, then this will benefit the right arm and left arm out swing bowler (the latter is inswing to the left-handed batter).

    - If the wind is coming in over mid off, then this will benefit the left arm orthodox bowler especially when the arm ball is attempted as well as right arm inswing and left arm inswing bowlers (the latter is outswing to the left-handed batter).

- Being aware of the movement and the effect of the sun. Where will it be in the second half of the game? Will it produce shadows? Is it significant?

- Being aware of possible/probable light conditions at a later point in the game. What time did it go dark the day before? Were the conditions similar?

- Interpreting how a pitch will play and predicting its consistency. Is it likely to be two-paced? Are there any green patches? Where is the rough? What are the pitch characteristics on a length, short of a length, over pitched etc?

Four methods are common:

A - Use of a key to determine the resistance to downward pressure.

B - Bouncing a cricket ball to see what rebound characteristics are present.

C - Using the fingers to press on the surface for firmness and to feel for moisture.

D - Observation of worn areas, grassy areas, cracks, and of neighbouring tracks to see if there are any "tell tale" wear patterns etc.

Care needs to be taken with A and B. The area where the ball is going to pitch should be avoided, but the method still gives a general idea of what might be expected.

- If the key goes easily all the way in, the pitch will usually be slow and low and require the "wheelie bin" technique described in the technique section earlier in this chapter. This will affect the strategy of both teams.

- Alternatively, at the other extreme, the key may not go into the surface at all, which usually indicates that the pitch will have consistent pace and often, but not necessarily, bounce.

- In another situation the top may be soft, but for there to be a hard layer just under the surface. This usually indicates that the ball, if bowled at the correct pace, will leave the pitch with a higher elevation than normal.

- And in another situation, the surface may be firm but with a lot of grass left on the pitch. The outcome is usually that lateral movement from seam bowlers can be expected.

- Lateral movement can also be predicted if the surface is

firm and moist, maybe because the pitch has been covered overnight. This frequently makes the grass "sweat" and usually assists with lateral movement. How long this lasts depends on the length of the grass and the speed that the pitch dries out due to the wind and sun.

- Though not "pitch", two other important factors need to be taken into account: cloud cover and temperature. Cloud cover can often assist swing bowling provided that the temperature isn't too cold, while warm and humid weather can also assist swing.

- Players are encouraged to watch television and to listen to pitch reports, because much useful information will be heard.

- Players are also encouraged to recognise that in most of these situations, there is a speed of ball, which is most effective in a particular set of conditions e.g. a ball will swing differently at different speeds (mph or kph) dependent on the prevailing conditions. Understanding this helps swing bowlers adjust in order to make the ball swing late. It's a case of finding the correct speed for that day. Another example would be with a spin bowler where the speed of delivery is vital in relation to the receptiveness of the surface to "bite".

- Recognition of the vital importance of the all rounder. Dent the confidence of an all-rounder in one area and it often transfers to the other.

- Targeting key opposition players. Their failure can have an enormous effect on the opposition team morale. Failure here means maybe depriving a batter of runs but also depriving a bowler of wickets. Knowing how key batters were dismissed in previous games or knowing the analysis of key bowlers in recent games can unearth factors that indicate what type of strategy to employ.

The list in all of the four areas above could go on and on, and could easily be the subject of a book on its own!

Useful resources for evidence:

Players often require evidence to persuade them that the tactical observation being made is sound. The sources of evidence can call upon:

- The observations of an individual player in a one-to-one situation
- The observations of members of the team in groups or as a team
- The observations of captain, vice-captain or senior player
- The observations of the coach

- The observations of the scorer.

The first four sources of evidence are almost certain to be subjective with some factual base, while the fifth source can be highly and more objectively significant.

In the absence of live footage of matches and the facility for in-depth analysis, the scorebook can be the club coach's most important provider of data; so good relationships with the team scorer are vital if you want the scorebook kept in a certain way. I like each bowler to be scored in a separate colour and for the balls a batter receives to be logged in colour. In this way, it is possible to track which bowler bowled to which batter with what outcome.

Through this method, it is easy to identify both strength and weakness. It can identify the bowlers that the batter appeared confident against. It also informs whether a batter had difficulty with a particular bowler, or went through a particularly difficult patch with two or more bowlers, or alternatively went through a difficult phase in an innings. The same can be applied to bowling. It is possible to identify the batter/s that a bowler was able to dominate as well as the batter/s, which caused a bowler more difficulty.

The pattern of a game can be read from the scorebook even more clearly if the "Bill Frindall" system is used, but in most cases the orthodox book can be good enough with the above colour and dot system. Not only can the contest between batter and bowler be tracked, but also, through plotting the run rate in a bar graph as used on television, the fall of wickets in relation to the target score achieved can be followed. This can give telling insights into the risk levels that were employed and can be extremely useful in proving that the risk levels were appropriate or that adjustments to the style of play are needed if similar circumstances repeat themselves. (See next page for an example that shows that the risk levels were not evenly spread in chasing a target score. The low early innings risk levels led to a higher run rate task in later overs and the higher risk levels required contributed significantly to the loss of wickets.)

Two examples in which the scorebook didn't lie

1. The team debrief should be brief and highlight the main tactical turning points of a game without undermining the authority of the captain. For example, when chasing a large target, there are frequently "magic" or "critical" moments when a particular over can change the course of a game. In the following real 45 over National Knock Out game, Wolverhampton were chasing a total of 214 and needed 104 off 16 overs to win. The run rate was over a run a ball (6.625) but after scoring 14 off the 30th over, it left Wolverhampton to score 90 off 15 overs

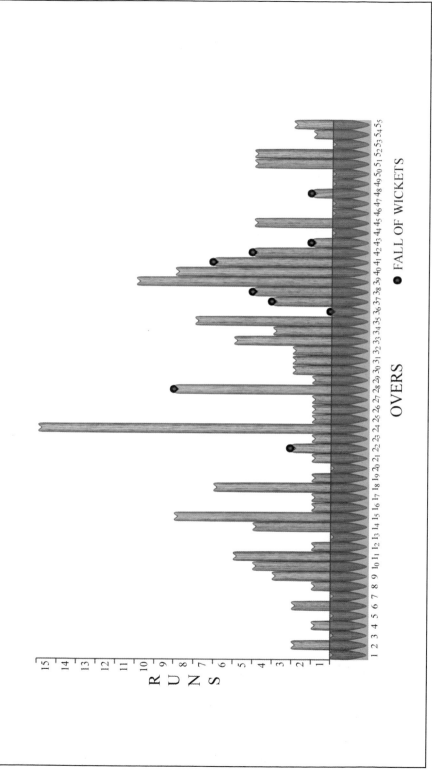

OVERS

● FALL OF WICKETS

or a run a ball (6.0). The run chase became more manageable and the match was won.

Pointing out the importance of the 30th over can develop the tactical thinking of the batters, bowlers and fielders. It gives an opportunity to congratulate the batters concerned for the vision they showed in raising the risk levels in that particular over rather than letting the run rate creep up to dangerous levels. The batters learn by recognising that risk levels sometimes have to be increased to regain balance in the run chase, while the bowlers and fielders recognise how important it is to keep a batting side in "jail".

2. In another match, again by co-incidence chasing a score of 214, Wolverhampton were in a strong position with an overseas opening bat firmly set when the second wicket fell. The opposition were under consideration and admitted after the game that they thought the game had gone away from them. The opposition however, recognised that the new batter, who was in his first season of premier league cricket, was playing at a low risk level. They therefore adopted a policy of giving the "set" batter a single early in the over and then setting a saving one field for the new batter. The bowling was also changed to bring an off spinner on because the new batter was left-handed.

The opposition strategy started to work because the measured and appropriate run rate started to evaporate. The "set" batter started to become anxious, and as a consequence started to raise his risk levels and became the next wicket to fall. The match was tied, but it was a match that should have been won. During the following week, it was possible to go through the game with the left-handed batter and to show where the crucial or missed "magic" moment had occurred. If the batter had either gone for short sharp singles or selectively taken the off spinner on and hit him over the top during that critical 6 over period of the game about two-thirds through the Wolverhampton reply, the opposition strategy would have been in disarray.

The other way to learn from the same experience is to emphasise what the opposition had done tactically so that players will recognise it when it arises again, or alternatively, can recognise it when their own captain uses the same tactics against an opposition team.

Over time and by analysing real match situations, it is possible to build up a kind of team understanding of how to play in certain circumstances. This is particularly important with a young side and is an effective method of making the most out of each experience. The main decision is whether to review the game immediately or to leave it for a practice session when all the players might not be present. Alternatively, one-to-one use can be made of the same match experience.

Examples 1 and 2 above both involved run chases. And one of the things young players often make errors of judgement over is risk level in relation to runs required. This sometimes has to be coached. One way I advocate for those players who have difficulty with the division involved in calculating required run rates is to agree with the other batter the rate required. Once this has been done, there is no need to recalculate after each over but merely to count + 1 or + 2 or -1, etc., depending on the runs scored in an over. In other words the player just tracks the discrepancy between run required and runs scored. Sometimes this discrepancy is + and at others times –. This enables the batters to assess the appropriate risk level that ensures that the batting side keep in touch with the required rate. This helped inform when the "magic moment" described in example 1 was needed.

Tactics in practice situations

The above two examples came as a result of specific match situations, but it is possible to simulate them in practice. It requires the coach to set up a square practice and to re-create the situation with fielders, bowlers and batters all playing a role.

Factors that the coach will bear in mind include anything from the earlier list of tactical team considerations to the rules of a particular competition. For example, the minimum number of overs for a game to count as a complete game (and not classified as abandoned when there is indifferent weather around), and the points system of the competition, can all have a bearing on the tactical dimension.

The coach sets the scene and then asks the players to respond in an active session. After the scenario has been played out for a while, a discussion can then be held as to how players responded. The outcome is hopefully greater tactical insight!

In a specific example, a coach may have worked on technically improving the running between the wickets in taking quick singles and emphasising the use of the bat as an extension of the arm, the use of a lower centre of gravity to make the arm and bat extend yet further and at the same time allow a quick spin on the feet and a quick drive off into the next run, etc. This could then lead into batters trying to take singles in a match scenario while bowlers and fielders try to stop the singles. This could then be added to by pairing batters who have been having problems running together. Problems can be solved on occasions by using humorous analogies to get the points across. An example might be that a player views his/her batting partner as being twice their normal weight because they are a poor judge of a run due to lack of anticipation. The question the coach is posing is "If that was the case (twice the weight) would you take that quick single or that two?" And the comment from the coach could be "Such a weight would be difficult to get moving, and similarly be like a barge in a lock - difficult to turn round." And "If you use this method you will be compensating in your decision making for the lack of anticipation in your batting partner". Discussion could then follow to see if this solved the running between the wickets difficulty. Carefully handled, the player who has difficulty with anticipation will not be offended, but understand the need to find a solution to run-outs when they are involved. This is an unusual example but it illustrates the point that the coach can simulate practically any match situation. An understanding of the above scenario could make the difference between winning and losing a match.

COMBINING THE MENTAL, TECHNICAL AND TACTICAL

Mature players need a mature approach and one method that can be used is what I call a 'Problem solving approach'. It requires a "questioning" style as opposed to a "telling" style. See chapter 4 - "Communication".

Examples that I have used include:

- "Batting on different surfaces" where upside down mats have kept the honeycomb uppermost. Putting two or even three mats on top of each other can produce slower and lower bounce simulations. Putting other smaller pieces of mat on top of the main mat can simulate rough.

- Developing strategies for such things as:

  "Bowling to left handed batters"

  "Taking poor throws for wicket keepers"

  "Batting against left arm bowlers"

  "Bowling at the tail"

The same method can be taken further with such problem solving examples as:

- "How to score effectively without raising risk levels too high"

- "Building up a strategy to play spin"

- "Bowling to a plan with an assessment of the risk levels involved"

By making it a problems solving approach, the player becomes fully involved and has some ownership over the strategies that are devised. Many more situations that combine an appreciation of the mental, technical and tactical could be constructed.

Captain and tactics

It is important that captain and coach talk about tactics. They may not always agree, but it is still important to have the discussion. It is the discussion itself, which helps to clarify the issues. The way a coach relates to the captain is dealt with in chapter 4, so I mention it only briefly here. The captain, in my opinion, should do most of the talking. By explaining his/her tactics to the coach, the captain clarifies his/her thinking.

The areas that might be discussed include:

- Batting order in a normal full length game
- Batting order if an early wicket falls
- Batting order to make best use of right and left-handed batters
- Batting order if quick runs are required near the end of an innings
- Batting order dependent on the bowling strengths of the opposition
- Which bowlers to be given the new ball
- Which bowlers to work in tandem - permutation of combinations
- Which bowlers to bowl from which end bearing in mind the playing surface, wind direction, the sun and light conditions
- Which bowlers to bowl to right and left-handed batters
- Which bowlers to bowl at the death.

Final thought in this section

It is possible for a coach to attempt to impart tactical wisdom in simulated situations and this can be a powerful learning tool, but in the end, it is real time match examples that provide the best opportunity to identify tactical factors from which the players can learn.

The tactical and technical "ingredients" are, at times, difficult to separate, and in my view should grow along parallel lines with talented players. Technical and tactical expertise can be developed, practised, seen to be appropriate and put to use in real match situations before either is fully mature. The coach should recognise that especially young players will make tactical mistakes, but that it is the constructive use of successful as well as unsuccessful match play that will lead a team towards improved understanding.

LIFESTYLE

A few things that relate to lifestyle were mentioned in the "Physical" section of this chapter, but before saying any more, it is important that what is understood by the word "Lifestyle" is clear at the onset. In some ways it is better described as "Lifestyle Management".

At the simplest level it would involve a focus of how active we are on a day-to-day basis and what we eat and drink. Diet is an often-misused word because its common use links it to losing weight, but diet really describes what enters the body via the mouth and is routinely consumed by way of food and liquid. A broader definition of "Lifestyle" is considered later.

The ECB advise young county squad players that preparation for performance, whether practice or match, requires food to be eaten in small amounts with drink consumed at regular intervals. It is emphasised that fatty food should be reduced and be replaced with complex carbohydrates (see below in recommended meals), and that the liquid should be consumed before, during and after the activity. It is particularly stressed that the body should be refuelled with carbohydrates and fluids as soon as possible after playing or practising.

When it comes to recommending meals, the above advice is more specific. Breakfast should include plenty of bread, cereals, jam or marmalade, fresh or tinned fruit and low fat yoghurt. Lunch should emphasise such things as sandwiches, jacket potatoes, rice or pasta dishes, with fruit and low fat yoghurt for desert, while tea should include a light carbohydrate meal to replenish stores. Stodgy cakes and biscuits should be avoided!

At club level it is not possible to impose a strict regime on the players, but it is still good practice for the coach to encourage sensible eating and drinking and to, in particular, encourage appropriate eating and drinking before a match or practice. (See earlier in this chapter in the sections on "dehydration" and "energy depletion")

Over time, the coach will learn more and more important and interesting facts that can enter into one-to-one discussion. Just one example is given now and it relates to how to calculate the fat content of foods. It has been said above and is now widely recognised that everyone, and especially performers in sport, need to watch how much fat they consume. Labels on foods however, can be confusing and sometimes worse, misleading.

This information about fats is not advocating that fats should be avoided altogether because fats are an essential part of a balanced diet. It's really saying, "be careful"!

It is generally agreed that optimal athletic performance, as well as disease prevention and good health, are best promoted when fat constitutes 30% or less of the calorific content of the food consumed. The question is how to work out that what is being eaten contains less than 30% fat. The information required relates to the **fat percentage in kilocalories (kcals)** in the food.

A description of how to work out an accurate fat percentage in kilo-calories can be found below, but this is too complicated for many players to think about on a routine basis unless a motivated player wants to seriously lose weight! So what's the easiest alternative? A general rule within the context of a balanced diet and in relation to an active lifestyle and one that is used as a "rule of thumb" by one major county cricket club is that players should avoid any product that contains more than **5 grams of fat per 100 grams of product.**

This might be a little high for the inactive, but is fine for the trained athlete. It also has to be recognised that everyone needs a treat in life at some time! It's when the treat becomes the norm that the lifestyle affects performance.

The context of the above "rule of thumb" is the trained athlete, while what follows is a guide for the club player who is likely to be less fit than a professional cricketer. If the percentage of the weight of the product is looked at, it can look healthy. It is important however to recognise that each gram of fat contains 9 kcals. The performer therefore needs to look at the number of grams per 100 grams of product, multiply this by 9 and see whether the product remains at 30 or below. You will be surprised how often the answer is above 30, e.g. whole milk approaching 50%!

Taking another example, a chicken burger, knowing that a lot of young players will probably eat convenience foods at some time during a week!

Chicken burger	per 100grams	= 238 kcals
Fat	13.5grams x 9	= 121.5 kcals

If the packet is only given a quick glance, 13.5 grams in 100 grams of chicken burger might appear appropriate. This refers to 13.5% of the weight of the product. It is not however 13.5% of the kcals. After multiplying the 13.5 by 9 the score rises rapidly to 121.5kcals. Now divide the 121.5 into 238 and the real percentage of fat content in kcals can be established. The answer is just over 51% or well above the recommended 30%.

An alternative way when selecting products is to look in the column "per serving". After reading the second line where the energy value in kcals is usually written, look lower down the contents list to make sure (ideally) that the grams of fat are about 3grams or below per 100kcals of energy. Take the example of a frozen and packaged "Healthy" chicken curry.

Chicken Curry	per meal cooked including rice
Energy	475kcal (Calories
Fat	8.4grams

The above would translate as follows. 475 kcals is four and a three-quarters of 100kcals, therefore divide 8.4 by 4.75 to find out the grams per 100kcals. The answer is just over 1.7 grams of fat, which is well within the 3-gram limit. Hope that you are not more confused than when you started.

After establishing that the fat content is acceptable, it is then a case of controlling the quantity of food consumed. Good homework can be lost quite easily if large quantities are consumed, so the total packet kcals value has to be considered as well as the per 100grams and kcals values.

If performers are to maintain a stable weight or to lose weight, where appropriate, then the small print has to be read and a few calculations carried out. It makes a difference over time.

The ECB Level II course includes in its Manual Supplement a section on food for cricket. Some of this supplement repeats the information above, but it also includes information on meeting the energy demands of cricket. It asks the question 'Why Carbohydrates?'. It then answers the question and lists carbohydrate sources, describes a balanced diet, and raises awareness of food and drink in general. There is a useful reminder of the effect of alcohol on performance, which is important for many players in England, as there is a culture that frequently associates drink and top club cricket. If top quality club cricket is what the coach and team wants, then perhaps this part of the culture needs to be visited and scrutinised!

Useful information that the coach might use on a one-to-one basis with individual players is that 21 units of alcohol are the recommended maximum for a male and 14 units for a female per week. It is further recommended in order to control daily drinking that men aim for no more than 3-4 units per day and women 2-3 units per day and that alcohol free days are incorporated into the week.

1 unit of alcohol is about 1 x 50ml measure of sherry, 1 x 100ml glass of wine, half a pint of beer or 1 x 25ml of spirits. Drinking at home is more difficult to control because measures will often be higher than those purchased at pubs or restaurants. The most accurate way of working out units however is to multiply the volume consumed by the percentage of alcohol and to the divide this by 1000. A coach might use this accurate measurement if a player confided to having something of a problem with drink. For example:

> 1 x 440 ml can of mild beer at 3.5% = 440 x 3.5
> = 1540 divided by 1000 = 1.54 units

> or 1 x 330 ml designer beer at 5.1% = 330 x 5.1
> = 1683/1000 = 1.68 units

The ECB Level III course develops what is meant by lifestyle beyond exercise and what we eat and drink, and includes consideration of three areas:

- Life outside cricket
- Life off the field
- Life on the field

'Life outside cricket' looks at "Personal Development" and how the education of players and a player's career needs to be planned. 'Life off the field' looks at "Professional Development" and looks at the essential support structures, while 'Life on the field' emphasises "Performance Development".

The Level III course applies this to a young professional who wants to make cricket a career, but the same structure can be valuable when coaching at top club level.

- It makes sense to take an interest in the personal careers of a squad. To be in touch with that side of their life might prove crucial in the way the player is handled in a particular situation.

- If the circumstances were appropriate, it makes sense to be aware of issues that may be relevant to young players in the squad who wants to make cricket a career - e.g. time management, goal setting, financial planning and communication skills

- It makes sense to be in a position to advise and support players, particularly young players, with issues that directly relate to their performance on the field. For the amateur, the emphasis in this area will be on knowledge of things such as drug abuse, alcohol/tobacco, first aid, nutrition, diet and injury prevention. Where appropriate coaching qualifications, player diaries and performance tracking, can also support individual development.

The above, while particularly relevant to the first class game can transfer to the top club game in specific circumstances. It's a case of picking out what is of value to particular individuals within a squad.

Like the other components in this chapter, it is not the function of the book to cover lifestyle in detail. There is a small amount of information here, but the coach needs to do more personal reading and to attend specialist courses if he/she wishes to acquire knowledge in depth.

One source of courses would be within the ECB coaching scheme where there are workshops that relate to lifestyle. A second would be the National Coaching Foundation (NCF), which also has a programme of workshops that the aspiring coach might find helpful. The NCF also produce a lot of useful literature.

One of the challenges for the coach is how to approach this area and how best to communicate lifestyle issues as a way of life without appearing to be giving a lecture! An informal source of information that I find useful, not only for myself, but also with players is the publication "Men's Health". It covers a wide variety of topics in an exciting, snappy, interesting way that appeals to men of all ages. Men for example who might brush the coach away if the coach tried to engage in a discussion about a lifestyle issue may well be persuaded to read an article in a fashionable publication.

I feel sure that the same principle can be transferred to women cricketers. Fashionable magazines can support the work of the coach. For men and women cricketers, the main task of the coach is awareness raising and the coach is recommended to leave every avenue open as a means of communicating the message.

FINAL THOUGHT FOR THIS CHAPTER

I've tried to think of an analogy to explain the importance of the five elements described in this chapter: physical, mental, technical, tactical and lifestyle management. It won't be original I feel sure, but if the coach imagines a five-legged stool, the weight of the person can only be supported properly if all five stool legs are present. It might be theoretically possible to balance on two or three out of the five legs but the stool would be highly unstable. When there is a relationship between the five legs however, and they are all in right place and securely connected to the seat, they provide a much stronger and stable foundation that can withstand significant stress. Well you know what I mean!

Taking the analogy further, the five-legged stool will still be unstable if the legs are of unequal length. The implication is clear. The coach needs to be developing expertise in all five areas. This chapter has hopefully provided the broad picture and a limited amount of detail in the five areas. It's now up to the individual coach to explore the avenues of knowledge that are appropriate as he/she attempts to become the balanced "all-rounded" coach.

COMMUNICATION : THE CRUCIAL FACTOR

Communication between people is complex, and distinguishing between the strength of different influencing factors is difficult and by its nature subjective. Everyone recognises a good communicator, and can probably describe the qualities the good communicator appears to possess, but it is the thought process behind the communication that remains the hardest to identify.

In the context of a cricket coach working with a largely amateur club side, I offer this personal and subjective perspective as one way of identifying the key factors that influence the players and the team. In order to avoid repetition, the reader will be frequently directed during this chapter towards examples that already exist within the book.

A cricket team or squad is made up of individuals, pairs and groups. Collectively they inter-relate in a complicated manner and it would be the job of a social psychologist to explain the dynamics of how the different parts interact. In this chapter however, I am going to look at it from a practical point of view and without theoretical background.

I see 5 main inter-relating factors at work when coaching a team or squad. The 5 circles represent the 5 factors when looked at in isolation. The circle, "Players including captain", is seen as separate from 'Team'. 'Team' is when the captain and players are performing as a cricketing unit in a match, whereas "Players including captain" is a description of 11 separate influential personalities in a group situation as people rather than cricketers.

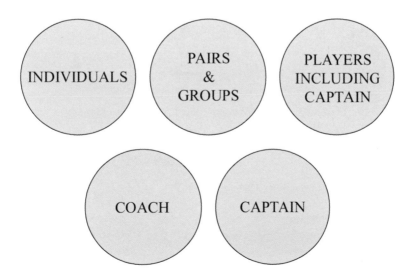

But what is the relationship between them? Are any of them more important than any other?

I believe that there are two major influencing factors in a top club side: the coach on the one hand and the captain and players on the other. The diagram below is an attempt to represent these two major influences and also indicate how they impact on individuals, pairs and groups and the team. The bottom part of the diagram is designed to indicate how crucial the relationship is between coach and captain and how that relationship feeds into and underpins the main channels of communication. If there is a quality relationship between coach and captain, and they share the same strategic vision, then their combined influence can be enormous.

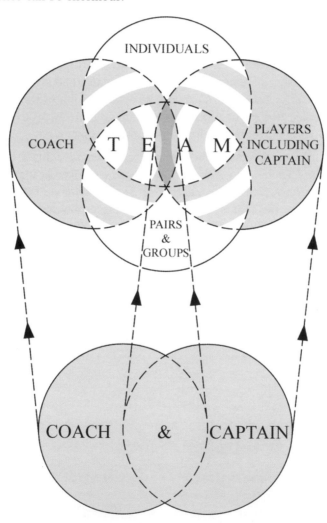

In the end, it is the team that matters and how they perform. The coach who has a strategy for recognising and managing these overlapping influences is likely to make fewer errors of judgement, and fewer errors of judgement is the hallmark of a quality manager (coach in this case).

Before moving on to describe examples of working with individuals, pairs and groups and the team, I would like to first of all reflect of what is involved in communication.

Communication can come in many forms. Face to face conversation can be enhanced by the appreciation of other forms of communication. Some are obvious while others come in disguise. The coach who is truly "on the ball" will be aware of most of them. In addition to assisting the coach's work with individual players some will enable the coach to analyse opposition players.

ECB level II coaches will be aware that communication is about:

- Talking and listening, and listening isn't just hearing!
- Sending and receiving information - the "what".
- Paralanguage, including the pitch, volume and speed with which words are spoken - the "how".
- Body language including facial expressions, gestures and body movement, body posture, spatial awareness and clothes and appearance.

There is expertise to be developed in all of the above areas and coaches and players are likely to favour one method rather than another. The coach however, will recognise the value in expanding their range of communicating styles. Two fascinating and most important facts, for example, are that over half of anyone's information comes through body language while almost a further 40% comes from how words are said rather than the words themselves. The implications are clear for the coach; there must be control in what non-verbal messages are sent and the ability developed to interpret the messages received.

Cricket is a highly visual game and so sensitivity to body language messages is a very important skill for the top club coach to develop. The skill will involve sensitivity to not only his/her own players, but also to the opposition. The body language on arrival, during warm ups and practices, during games and socially after the game can all be informative. It can start with simple tactical observations during a warm up before a match, which identify whom in the opposition is left-handed or right-handed, and who appears to bat and whether they play straight, or bowl off spin or seam, where this is not known from previous encounters, and who appears to have a good arm etc.

It moves on from there to include an assessment of the mental state of players on both sides. Careful observation can frequently identify, for example, such issues as confidence, over-confidence or lack of confidence. The coach will also be aware of the information that his/her team give to the opposition through body language and will try to ensure that the team always send out positive messages whatever the recent form of the team. The most important body language communication however, is during the match when fielders, bowlers and batters communicate so much about their thinking.

The ECB level II course considers how coaches relate to players and stresses the importance of communicating in positive language and of finding ways to surround any critical or corrective feedback with praise. This recognises human nature and the fact that acknowledging qualities in a player's performance is likely to make the same player receptive to advice. The same course helps coaches to understand and develop their own communication effectiveness.

I fully subscribe to the guidelines that are suggested and describe a few in my own words.

Credibility is vital if effective communication is to take place. Players will only listen once they have accorded credibility to the coach. The process starts with the coach using simple jargon free language and non-verbal as well as verbal interaction. If the coach is then able to combine the ability to be consistent, sincere and positive in the context of a "know your stuff" image, then credibility and respect are likely to be the bi-products. In the end, there is no substitute for a coach "knowing his/her stuff".

Working with top club players needs to emphasise **dialogue** and the coach who learns to listen can achieve this. Empathy with the player will help. I suggest that you would be more likely to communicate with someone else if the person you were talking to is attentive, didn't interrupt, helped you to express what you were trying to say by finding the word you were looking for when needed, or summarised what you had said to aid clarity and asked you questions. Very few people react negatively if they are asked questions and invited to give their opinions as opposed to being "told".

The ECB Level III course takes the **"questioning"** approach further, in the context of **feedback** being the key to success. I believe strongly that there is no learning without feedback. Sometimes the feedback comes from self-analysis or awareness, but frequently the process needs guidance and that is where the perceptive coach becomes active. The quality player who already has significant insight into what the game of cricket is all about, will often be able to pick up on the important issues quickly. The coach only needs to make a small steer in order to point the player in the right direction.

A number of the above points need to be used when it gets to practical one-to-one work with players. Questions need to be open-ended and might include something like the following after the completion of the game. "How do you rate your performance today?" "What were the best aspects - the parts you were pleased with?" "Are there any areas of your game that you feel could have been better?" "What were they?". By starting from this position, the ownership of the discussion is with the player. The discussion is trying to identify areas of agreement and areas in which dialogue would benefit the player. The coach then has the task of deciding how to express his/her input. In many cases the coach might well be saying something like, "Do you think in that situation it might have been a good idea to have...?". The coach is inviting comment rather than telling the player what they should have done in a situation. The coach is recognising that while he/she has a viewpoint, the player may have an equally valid viewpoint.

For a younger and less experienced player, it might be a mixture of questions and **"tell"**. At some point the coach might follow up some open-ended questions and decide that specific advice is appropriate. The coach might say something like, "In that situation it would have been a better idea to have...". The skill in this case is the judgement of the coach in choosing the appropriate route.

In another situation, even with players that normally meet the coach in quality dialogue, there is sometimes the need for the coach to "tell". The sort of example I am thinking of is when a player is out of form and is lacking in confidence. In situations like this, the player frequently doesn't want the responsibility of identifying the cause of problem, but wants an objective assessment as to what appears to be the trouble. If this happens, the coach puts the normal approach to one side and pinpoints possibly in the following manner. "At the moment you are..."(and then describes what has been observed). "What I think you need to do is..." (and then describes the 'solution' or 'alternative solutions'). In a short while, it will be possible to revert to the dialogue style once the temporary situation has been resolved or at least understood.

The Level III course explores the advantages and disadvantages of the "questioning" and "tell" approaches in more detail. However, at top club level, I strongly advocate dialogue and "questioning" because one of the objectives of the coach is to make the players as self-sufficient as possible.

Questions that start with **"What"**, **"Who"**, **"How"** and **"When"** are usually more successful, especially when they are wide-ranging and not too specific. Once the player has established the context, the coach can then gradually funnel the questions to pinpoint the key area or areas, and at the same time ensure that the player is centre stage at all times.

The same strategies can be applied to other situations involving more than one player.

The complex web of relationships that the coach needs to understand

I would like to repeat what was implied at the beginning of this chapter in the diagram, that the coach is not only involved with individual players, because individual players also belong to pairs, groups and of course the team. A cricket club is a complex organisation, but out of all the relationships that exist, the five main avenues of communication are, I believe:

- Between player and player
- Between the coach and the individual player
- Between the coach and pairs or small groups
- Between the coach and the team
- Between the coach and the captain

The above are the main drivers when it comes to performance on the field of play, although it is recognised that committee, selectors, club captains where that is different from the 1st team captain, ground maintenance team, etc, still have a bearing on success.

In the first category when the team are on the field, there are between the eleven players 55 separate relationships. If the coach is included, this rises to 66. The squad however, is not just 11 players and so the relationships between the whole squad are also very important. In a squad of 17, for example, there are 136 separate relationships, and if the coach is included this rises to 153.

In the second category, the coach has as many relationships as there are players in the squad – and this could quite easily be as high as 17 in a top club side – even though some of the relationships might only affect fringe players.

In the third category where the coach has a dialogue with pairs of players and small groups, there will again be a lot of combinations, and of course, in the fourth category (the team) there is one large group of maybe as many as 18 including coach and players who are involved in large group dynamics.

The task of the coach is therefore highly complex and highly skilled and friction in such a complex structure is bound to arise on occasions. Success on the field makes the job easier, but underachievement within a team or squad can create divisions that can be very difficult to handle. I will be concentrating on the second, fourth and fifth categories with reference made to the other two.

COMMUNICATION BETWEEN PLAYER AND PLAYER

It was mentioned above that there were 55 relationships on the field of play within one team (66 with coach) and 136 (153 with coach) in a squad of 17. This has implications for the management of a team or squad.

Refer to chapters 2 and 5 for a diagram, which shows what 66 relationships looks like when it is illustrated graphically. There is also more information in chapters 2 and 5 as to how this diagram can be used in communication with players in a team setting.

When it comes to the management of relationships/communication within a team and between players, it doesn't matter whether it is pre-season, practice or match play. The key question is whether the coach can have any effect on the quality of player-to-player communication. And the answer is yes.

A coach can't make players like each other, but he/she can make it quite clear that the expectation is that everyone in the team must have a working relationship with every other player in the team. Friction between players is damaging and must be prevented although a healthy exchange of views is desirable. Every squad of players will be different, but there are a number of things that a coach can do that can make a difference. There isn't one specific practice that can achieve a strong working relationship, but they can be developed by the way the coach works with the squad.

For example, if the coach allows players to decide the groupings in which they practice, then cliques can easily develop. While it is natural that players gravitate towards players they like or feel comfortable with, this could result in little contact with other players except when a match was being played. Older players and younger players can sometimes make it feel like two separate groups, while the debutant can easily be made to feel ill-at-ease when changing room space is zealously guarded or they are not made welcome but ignored.

Ways in which some of this can be avoided relate to the organisation of practice. It starts with the coach working out some groupings that will need to work together when it comes to matches. It might be pairs of bowlers or the first four batters, or the fielders who "save one" or the wicket keeper and the slips/close catchers, or etc. The pairs of bowlers, for example, might on occasions be both pace, but there are going to be match situations when pace and spin will work in tandem, and it's that sort of flexibility and vision that will determine grouping decisions.

What I am recommending is that when a coach sets up practice situations, one of the factors that will be taken into consideration is finding ways of ensuring that players work with each other. If players, out of choice, or without thinking, avoid contact with another player, then the coach can orchestrate a practice situation in which they have to work together.

As part of an overall coaching strategy, this can have a significant effect (see team communication later).

COMMUNICATION BETWEEN THE COACH AND THE INDIVIDUAL PLAYER

As this section is read, I would stress the same point as was made on the first page of chapter 3 when talking about "The Vital Ingredients" of physical, mental, technical, tactical and lifestyle management, that players and the coach can bring moods or emotional states of mind to the both practice and matches. To ignore this fact can potentially lead to difficulties in both relationships and communication. It is the job of the coach to overcome any of his/her personal difficulties and to concentrate on adapting to the needs of the players.

There is no substitute for quality one-to-one communication between player and coach. Team communication is important, but it is the more personal one-to-one that, in my opinion, makes the difference. In a one-to-one situation, players are generally prepared to engage in a dialogue, which identifies the areas that are strong and the areas that need to be improved. The players in a one-to-one are also more likely to accept advice from the coach or to work with him/her to tackle the challenges presented. Frequently the same players will not accept to themselves the need when it is discussed in an open forum or in front of peers, although taking personal responsibility in a team setting is a very important attribute for a team to develop.

Communication between coach and player can be broken down into three phases:

- Winter leading up to pre-season
- Practice
- Match play

Winter leading up to pre-season and the individual player

After the players have had their end of season rest, I look for opportunities to meet individual players. This usually takes place after Christmas but on occasions it is before. In a sense, the ideal time would be before Christmas so that there is a gradual build up in preparation to the beginning of the season in April.

Although it isn't possible to meet face to face with all players, I try to have contact with all of the first team squad. The younger players are keen to engage in formal reviews while the more experienced players are more likely to prefer an open-ended discussion.

The "Player Review" pro-forma that I use is kept on computer. A copy is reproduced on the next page.

The player review example I would like to give relates to the time between the 1999 and 2000 seasons and essentially invites the player to make comments about their cricket in four areas:

- Where were you at the beginning of 1999?
- What went well during 1999?
- What would you like to improve?
- What do you need to do to improve and to be ready for the 2000 season?

Players are encouraged to make comments that refer to "Physical" (P), "Mental" (M), "Technical" (Te), "Tactical" (Ta), and "Lifestyle" (L) issues.

Chapter 3 reinforced the fact that the above areas were frequently overlapping, and the coach needs to remember this during a discussion. Organisation of the information expressed by the player is important.

The method used is to take a large piece of cardboard - something like the liner of a sizeable parcel - and to organise five vertical columns and five horizontal columns. The framework below is the updated 2000/2001 version.

	Physical	Mental	Technical	Tactical	Lifestyle
Where were you at the beginning of 2000?					
What went well during 2000?					
What would you like to improve?					
What do you need to do to improve and to be ready for the 2001 season?					
Anything else?					

It can be set out quite informally as it is only a mechanism for recording information at this stage.

Comments can refer to "Physical" (P), "Mental" (M), "Tactical" (Ta),
"Technical" (Te) or "Lifestyle" (L) issues.

Where were you at the beginning of 2000?

What went well during 2000?

What would you like to improve?

What do you need to do to improve and to be ready for the 2001
season?

Anything else?

CHAPTER FOUR

Comments can refer to "Physical" (P), "Mental" (M), "Tactical" (Ta), "Technical" (Te) or "Lifestyle" (L) issues.

Where were you at the beginning of 2000?

- 98 best yr. with bat, fielding up to scratch, confident about bowling prospects for 99 (all)
- Although mentally confident, still a gap with physical where I was one of the fittest (M & P)
- 98 England u15 "A" captain gave confidence but W'ton performance not as hoped (All)
- Tried "too hard"? Confident in own age group but trying to prove? at older age groups (M)
- England U16 during winter Fitness 12.00 on bleep test (P)
- Confident about prospects with U17 Staffs as opening bat & 2/1st team with W'ton (M)

What went well during 2000?

- Averaging 44.1 in all senior cricket (12 matches) in context of GCSE/Staffs commitments (all)
- Pleased with Staffs U17's Aver: 20/25 & used opportunity better at higher level, played important role in a number of difficult situations. 2-day cricket helped tactically (Ta, Te, & M)
- Confidence maintained until close to end of season (M)
- Established myself as fellow player not a "youngster". (M)
- Maintained technically high standards (Te)
- Maintaining physical fitness - 12.3 on bleep (P)
- Maintaining appropriate balance between cricket//academic study//family

What would you like to improve?

- Better performance in senior cricket & to be less affected by management decisions (M)
- Using feet/moving out to play, maintaining set-up balance & more weight through drives (Te)
- Bleep scores from 12.3 to between 12.5&13.0 (P) and strengthening upper body (P)
- Maintaining confidence levels on a high & getting out of "dips" quickly (Te & M)
- Develop captaincy thinking (M)
- Opportunities to lift confidence through "Counties" asking me to play (M)
- Content of CV to be sent to "Counties" (M & L)

What do you need to do to improve and to be ready for the 2001 season?

- 3 x 3 mile runs in 30 minutes max and reducing. (P)
- Consider use of stairs (13 steps) 5xu&d (walk) 5xu&d (jog/walk) 10xu&d (jog)+stretches (P)
- Develop upper body strength. Tone to start, then Nigel Stockill to help with programme (P)
- Read "Playing Better Cricket" (£9.99 from "Coachwise", Leeds) (Ta, M, L & P)
- Read about mental game plans for captains (M)
- Work on using feet, moving out, set-up and driving power (Te)

Anything else?

- To contact JDM (coach) if England & Staffs don't meet need.

CHAPTER FOUR

The venue for the discussion will have been agreed and chosen by the player, as this gives ownership of the process to the player. General non-specific "chat" will precede the process in order to establish a relaxed atmosphere in which trust is present.

It is not a good idea to ask for specific answers to the boxes above as this constrains the integral nature of the "Vital Ingredients". Although it varies from player to player, it usually works better if the invitation is given to include (P), (M), (Te), (Ta), and (L) but to concentrate on the answer to the question and not the five areas. I say something like, "I will do the recording. Don't worry about staying within tight boundaries. The mind doesn't work like that; it darts from place to place. So let it flow and I will put your answers into the appropriate categories."

Armed with a pack of the smallest "Post-it" stickers, the discussion is started. As the answers to the first question unfold, they can be scribbled onto a "Post-it" and placed in the appropriate column. If one of the five areas is left out, it is then that the coach can intervene to ask the player more specifically if there is anything in that area that they would like to say.

If the point being made by the player isn't clear to the coach, the coach can paraphrase what he/she thinks is being said in order to clarify.

When all of the questions have been asked and answered, the coach runs through the points that have been made in order to be sure that the answers have been correctly interpreted.

After the discussion has ended, I return to the computer and the "saved" template and type in the agreed points, and save it under the player's name. Two copies are printed off: one which I keep in a file along with other players reviews, and the other for the player. The process in effect creates an action plan for development within a specific timeframe. It also provides the background for more specific goals to be agreed where this is appropriate. Finally it provides a focus for the player in what should be a motivational process. A copy of a completed review for 1999/2000 can be found on the previous page. It is for a young player in the first team squad who was trying to break into the first team.

The successful dialogue between the coach and the player can be well illustrated if Michael Parkinson and his successful "Parkinson" interviewing technique on television are observed. There will be much more involved in his technique, but the key lessons that I think can be learned are:

- Homework is vital. Know as much as you can about the person you are having an interview/dialogue with

- Take a few calculated risks, to tease out information

- Have prepared questions to hand that can move the discussion into a new area

- Crucially, feed on the answer to a question when constructing the next question.

It is the last skill, when applied to a coach/player relationship, which can lead to a player identifying for him or herself what is required.

Once the player review has been completed and agreed, the coach can then start to devise methods of helping the player to meet their identified development needs. It is now that the areas within physical, mental, technical, tactical and lifestyle management can be addressed. For example, things in the mental area like the "Mental Skills Questionnaire", or "Performance Profiling", or the "List of Qualities I Possess" or "List of Achievement Reminders" etc. can be introduced as appropriate. On occasions, it is beneficial to the individual player to carry out questionnaires and profiling etc. before the review, in order to inform their self-assessment.

Practice and the individual

Practice is of two types: indoors pre-season and outdoors during the season.

It was said in chapter 2 in the section on pre-season preparation that the emphasis is likely to be on technical consolidation and improvement although the areas of physical, mental and tactical preparation will be in the mind of the coach (see the tactical section in chapter 3). Lifestyle issues at this stage will be managed on an individual basis, while individual player review objectives will also be worked on at this time.

It would be possible to give examples of working with an individual in the pre-season build-up to the season, but I have chosen instead to emphasise an example of working with an individual player in a "typical" practice session as described in chapter 2. The emphasis I would like to place here is in how a coach can influence a player during the season, and the example I am going to give relates to the development of the concentration level of a player through communication between coach and player, which resulted in the bowler entering the "zone of concentration".

I remember this particular practice; because it was the first time that I had coached a player who I recognised had entered the "zone". It made me realise that entering the "zone of concentration" was something that could be practised if a player was prepared to commit enough energy to it.

The method that was communicated was the same as in chapter 3 in the "Mental" section when it was applied to a one-to-one coaching situation where the routines of *see*, *do* and *say* concentration triggers were described.

The player, an all-rounder who was working on his bowling, started by saying that he was concerned that he was regularly spraying the ball down the leg side. Resisting the temptation to seek a technical solution, I decided instead to explore concentration as the potential missing factor.

The communication went something along the following lines, and it was accompanied by the use of body language, in particular the hands.

"I would like you to first of all concentrate on a run up which feels smooth, balanced and rhythmical."

Several balls followed with this objective in mind.

"At the start of your run up, your attention is at a quarter to three on the clock and the first task is to get your concentration to ten minutes to two, so looking down the pitch and *seeing* the batter or wicket keeper start his pre-delivery routine will achieve that."

"Decide which pre-delivery movement you are going to use (batter or wicket keeper) and practise a few balls focussing your attention on the same 'trigger'."

I used my hands to indicate the narrowing of the clock hands and several balls followed with this in mind.

"Now I want you to take the concentration from ten minutes to two, to five minutes to one, so after you have used the *seeing* 'trigger', I want you to *do* something with the ball, the same thing every time." We talked about one or two *doing* things that could be practised and settled on a deliberate placement of the fingers on the seam in the appropriate grip for the intended delivery. To keep it simple, we kept to the same type of delivery for each ball during practice. The hands were again used to indicate the narrowing of the clock hands.

Several balls followed with this in mind.

"Now I want you to take the concentration from five minutes to one to one minute either side of 12 o-clock, so after you have used the *seeing* and the *doing* trigger, I want you to *say* something to yourself, the same thing every time."

We talked about one or two things that could be said and settled on 'concentrate on off stump'. The hands were again used to indicate the tight focus that was required.

Several balls followed with this in mind

The practice was intense and both player and coach knew that something unusual and special was going on, and we took the practice situation one stage further.

"I want you to bowl an over in which you decide what you are going to bowl next on your way back to your mark, and then follow the 'triggers'.

The player did exactly that and bowled absolutely beautifully with great accuracy and consistency and without a hint of leg side bowling.

The practice was going so well I decided to take it still further and to deliberately try and distract the bowler by talking across his run up line to another player who I asked to talk back to me.

The player was so much in the "zone of concentration" that he didn't even notice that we were talking!

The player took this special experience with him into the next match, and reported back that it had made an enormous difference to both his concentration and his motivation.

The above is an example, but it shows how the coach can make significant strides forward with players without compromising or even mentioning technique.

Final thought in this section on communication between coach and player in practice, relates to the awareness of the coach to the performances of the previous weekend. The quality coach can empathise with both success, and perceived lack of it, with equal sensitivity. Different players need handling in different ways, and the player reviews mentioned earlier will have helped the coach to "know the player".

Match play and the individual

It is difficult to separate the individual from the team when it is applied to match play. The distinction I draw is that when I work with an individual player on an aspect that is primarily personal to that player, it is "match play and the individual". When the aspect is primarily connected with the tactics of winning a game, then I call that "match play and the team".

The example I give in this category is of a first team teenager batter who was working on a strategy for 'coping with sledging'. There will have been prior discussion between coach and player about the problem. The context may be that the opposition in the next match have a reputation for 'sledging'. The first thing to establish is if the player knows why 'sledging' exists. Some players need it to be pointed out that it is a deliberate distraction devise that is designed to break concentration.

As a coach, I don't like sledging, but it occurs, and players have to be prepared for it. The conversation with the player would go along the following lines.

"As a player you have several alternatives as to how to cope with 'sledging'. You can take the opposition player(s) on and make it six of one and half a dozen of the other, you can make a joke of it, you can at the other extreme say absolutely nothing and appear not to have heard anything or you can have such focussed concentration that you don't hear the words that are spoken. Everyone is different and players cope in different ways. You must make your own decision as to what is right for you. The main thing is that you have a strategy, which avoids just drifting into the match. Be prepared and know what you are going to do."

It could be that a practice had been specially constructed, prior to the match, to work on 'sledging'. The coach or a designated player would have been asked to play the role of the "sledger". Alternatively, it could be that the player had been asked in their preparation for a match to visualise the situation of 'sledging' and to imagine coping with it successfully.

On match day, the skill of the coach determines what is said to the player about the issue. It would be, depending on the player, generally to stick with their game plan. This example is designed to show that in match play, the coach has one-to-one communication in areas of a player's game that the rest of the team will know little or nothing about.

On the more general point when working with individuals in match play, chapter 5 gives a flavour of the roles that a coach may be required to play in the section that relates to "The day of the match" - the National Club Championship Final. This included knowing who to speak to and who to leave alone, who responds to eye contact and a nod of understanding, who needs specific advice, who needs picking up, who needs praise, who needs support, etc.

There is one more important relationship when considering communication between the coach and the players: communication between the coach and the professional or overseas player. Chapter 5 refers to this from the point of view of meeting as soon as possible and establishing how you are going to work together. Likewise, Chapter 3 (in the section 'Mental') adds some other factors that relate to the overseas player and communication. It is, I believe, important that a special relationship is forged which recognises the special responsibilities and expectations that this player has to shoulder. Sharing more details about the strategies you are employing is one way in which the coach is likely to obtain a positive response from the paid player.

COMMUNICATION BETWEEN THE COACH AND PAIRS OR SMALL GROUPS

There is less here that can be done pre-season in planning terms, so this area is best broken down into two phases:

• Practice

• Match play

Practice and pairs or groups

The concentration practice described earlier that led to him entering the 'zone' was with an individual bowler, but the methods could equally be used with a pair or a group in a practice situation. Similarly, the practice and match play issue of, for example, 'sledging' can be dealt with in pairs and groups in practice. Any number of practices could be devised for bowlers, batters and fielders that simulate match requirements. The limitation again is only the imagination of the coach. Here is one example from fielding that requires good communication between the coach and the players.

The communication would start with the pair or group working on the **saving-one** skill listing what is required to be effective in that position. This could be written on paper although it is most likely to be through discussion. This informs the coach as to what things are being taken into account. Discussion then follows to widen the scope of issues that need to be added.

Simulated practice situations can then be set up or match practice introduced to bring the skills to life. Logically, practice drills would be devised to emphasise technique to start with, and then expand to include the mental and tactical dimensions.

The above might not sound much, but what it does do is engage players in developing expertise in a specialist fielding position. Without a strategy of this kind, then players may be left to develop their specialist skill through trial and error. The example involves 'saving one' but it can be applied to any group of fielding positions that have common characteristics - slip fielders, close catchers, saving two, etc.

While it is possible for a coach to set up drills that will improve technique, appreciation of mental and tactical aspects require communication and simulated practice. The quality team in the field doesn't just happen. It has to be planned. For the coach to be effective in this area the coach and team need to agree who is going to specialise in what positions and then to work in units to share insights and develop expertise.

And the point made earlier is repeated to reinforce that it is in "practice" that the coach can orchestrate the pairs and groups that work together to ensure that all players have contact with each other over a period of time.

Match play and pairs or groups

Communication can be prepared fully with the players who are either going to open the batting or open the bowling. The scorebook contains no details at this stage, although this situation doesn't last long before reactive tactical decisions have to be made. As the game develops, the skill of deciding what tactics to employ becomes more and more important and the intervention of the coach can be highly significant as the game unfolds.

The coach will draw on his/her own experience to decide whom to talk to and when. If for example, the opening batters put on a good partnership, the coach may well bring batters 3, 4 and 5 together to discuss the shape of the game and the appropriate tactics for the next phase should a wicket fall.

It is not possible to say exactly how "communication events" would occur with players or groups of players because it depends so much on the individuals concerned, but in the example above, it may well be appropriate to bring batters 6, 7 and 8 together (and maybe more) to inform them of the current thinking. This ensures that all players are kept involved even though their contribution is some distance away. This is particularly beneficial with younger and less experienced players.

Communication with existing batters is more difficult although drinks breaks create an opportunity. Otherwise the main route for communication is after the fall of a wicket via the incoming batter, which makes it all the more important that the incoming batter knows what the objectives of the next phase of play are. Communication with pairs and groups will be restricted when the team are in the field and may only be possible at a drinks break, so what is said before going onto the field is important and clear vision from the captain is important. (See the fifth avenue of communication below, between coach and captain)

COMMUNICATION BETWEEN THE COACH AND THE TEAM

As with the communication between the coach and the individual, it can be broken down into three phases:

- Winter leading to pre-season
- Practice
- Match play

Winter leading up to pre-season with the team

I am not proposing to repeat the examples that already exist in the book. The reader is referred to chapter 2 'Preparation' - "The Heart of Success", when, in the example prior to the 1999 season, a consultation meeting with players focussed on "What have we got to do to repeat the success of the 1998 season". It describes a process that led to 5 agreed priorities. The role of the coach was to manage the discussion and the outcome.

There is another example in chapter 5 'Match Action' - "Making Things

Happen" when a players meeting was arranged to "Exorcise the ghost" after a season of underachievement that narrowly kept Wolverhampton in the top flight! In this case the object of the meeting was to reflect on the season and to identify the main reasons for the underachievement. It was designed to clear the air, so that the 2001 season could be approached with new confidence and determination.

The key to a successful meeting with a team is planning. The ECB Level III course spends some time on how to prepare for meetings between the coach and individuals, pairs and small groups and teams. The team meeting is the most difficult to plan as it needs to take into account so many factors including age, experience and personality.

The essentials of a well-planned team meeting are:

- Be clear what your **objective** is. What do you want to achieve?

- Plan and **structure** the meeting to keep within the time limits available. The professionalism you bring to the meeting will communicate to the team. The planning is a non-verbal method of communication quite separate from the meeting itself.

- "Bounce" your **ideas** off someone else before "jumping in"

- **Discuss with captain and vice-captain** when it concerns the development of agreed team targets and performance goals. Their role will be crucial in the meeting. In some cases the coach and captain will work in tandem on an agreed and discussed agenda.

- Recognise that team meetings imply **interaction, involvement and participation**. The players are not present to be talked at although there is still and opportunity for clear expectations to be communicated from coach and captain.

- **Distinguish between** the point above and a **team talk prior to a match** when the coach and/or captain will be the main speaker

- Recognise that you are looking for a **response from the players** and that this implies a quality introduction to the meeting. Is the subject under discussion one that will easily obtain a response or is it something that will need significant input first. For example, introducing the concept of "Performance Goals" will need careful handling.

- Decide how much **time** is going to be spent as a **whole group** and how much time as **individuals, pairs or small groups**. From what you will have read or will read elsewhere, you will have noted that I am a fan of working in pairs, as long as the pairs are not always the same. Sometimes, working in small groups can add variation and prevent the boredom that can come from repetition.

- Decide how you are going to **record outcomes** - flip chart?

• Decide **how, or if,** you are going to **publish the outcomes**.

The outcome of good planning is that the coach is likely to receive a constructive contribution from the players, and a constructive contribution from the players is much more likely to lead to shared and agreed objectives.

In terms of communication with the players, it is important to start any meeting off on the right foot. One effective way is to make it clear what the agenda for the meeting is designed to cover and to ensure that 'any other business' is present on that agenda in order to leave room for questions/comments from players on other issues.

In a pre-season meeting, which for example is designed to focus on teams goals and performance targets, it helps to have a few items with which to warm the squad up to the task. One such item is to refer to the playing conditions for the coming season, especially when there has been change. Chapter 5 emphasises the importance of this in the circumstances when a team is underachieving and relates it to points lost when players have an incomplete understanding of the playing conditions.

Practice and the team

Practice with the whole team is difficult to achieve for the amateur club. The chance of all of the team that played on the previous Saturday league match being able to attend the next midweek practice is slim. (See chapter 2 on the challenges of running a "Routine" or "Normal" practice evening, and later in the same chapter, changes in circumstances, which alter the routine or normal practice.) The coach, therefore, has the task of deciding whether to deal with some matters that arose out of the previous match with some players only, or deal with some matters knowing that one-to-one discussion would have to fill in the gaps for the absent players, or postpone discussion and make the comments at the beginning of the next match.

The decision of the coach is much easier if the team are playing well and are generally winning - any of the three methods would be appropriate. Team communication in these circumstances can be left to the next match because it will be more a case of reinforcing the positive messages that the players can see are working. Communication on the practice night is more likely to be one-to-one and focus on individual players contribution to the previous match.

The decision of the coach is more difficult if the practice follows an indifferent performance. The danger with the option of leaving the team talk to the next match is that it might dwell on potential team and individual "baggage". In these circumstances, I think it better to cover the main issues with those that are at practice and to catch up with one-to-one with those that are absent. This might even be carried out on the 'phone. In this way, it makes it possible for the coach to be upbeat and positive in the pre-match communication.

In exceptional circumstances, it might be appropriate for the coach to communicate with the team in writing. One such example is recounted in chapter 5 when things were going wrong in the league and time was running out. It was after match 17 when only 5 matches remained to rescue the situation.

Sometimes, the coach and captain decide that the main issues are too important to be dealt with in this way. And if this arises, a team meeting may have to be called. This would happen infrequently, and focus on obtaining an agreed strategy out of the meeting. The example that follows tries to pursue this line of thinking.

As a result of the events of the 2000 season, I have prepared a unit on "Control the controllable" that I can use with the team if it becomes appropriate. In the 2000 season I listed the factors which were out of control for the players, but with hindsight, I think a more rounded explanation/discussion would have be beneficial. This is how I would approach it now. (Chapter 5 describes the team talks for the 2000 season with matches 3 and 8 relevant because they focused on "Controlling the controllable") I recognised, as coach, that the players were:

1. Attributing blame to factors which were outside their control

2. Avoiding taking personal responsibility for their own actions

If this happens again, this is what I propose to do:

• Create an opportunity to discuss the issues

• Use a prepared flip chart

• Involve the players in discussion

• Achieve two end products: greater player understanding of what is happening within the team and greater willingness of players to take personal responsibility.

The flip chart would look something like tthe table overleaf. It's based on Weiners' model of causal attribution (6).

It is based on an example used in an ECB Level III course, when "attribution" is discussed in some detail. Attribution sounds a fancy word, but it simply means - 'To what do the players attribute the success or failure of the team or their own performance' or 'where do the players lay the blame!'

	INTERNAL "Within the players control"	**EXTERNAL** "Outside the players control"	
STABLE "Predictable"	Talent/Ability	Coaching Task difficulty	**STABLE** "Predictable"
UNSTABLE "Unpredictable"	Effort Form Preparation Practice Psychological Factors	Luck Umpires Weather Pitch condition	**UNSTABLE** "Unpredictable"

The framework and the words in bold above would be on the flip chart, and underneath the words in italics would be listed. They would be in a random order. The discussion would seek to highlight the predictable and unpredictable, and those factors that are within or outside the players control. If the brief meeting brought about some reflection on the part of the players and better still a change of attitude that led to more focus on the factors "Within the control" of the players, then the meeting would have been worth while.

Match play and the team

Chapter 5 contains information, which relates to three different and contrasting examples of coach/team situations. There are specific 'team talk' examples on "what" was said in pre-match talks for a top of the table clash and also the last match of the 1998 season when the Birmingham and District Premier Cricket League was won; on "what" was said during the National Club Championship matches from regional final to the final at Lord's which was won in 1999; and on "what" was said in team talks during 2001 in the Birmingham and District Premier Cricket League when survival became the objective.

The above examples recount the "what" in information terms. It is in effect communication at the preparation stage. The references do not indicate "how" the information was delivered or what methods were used to ensure that the delivery was effective, although the pre-match briefing four days before the National Club Championship Final in 1999 probably came closest to giving a flavour of the communication methods I use. (See chapter 5)

When the spirits of a team are down, the communication from the coach has to be upbeat. Acting in a theatrical and inspirational way helps, but there are no short cuts to powerful delivery other than practice and experience. Even when the team are performing well, the coach needs to consider carefully how the message is going to be delivered. The coach is always on show and needs to play the role of an actor/actress who is performing in a relatively small room environment. This is a presentational skill and doesn't mean that the message is insincere just because it is transmitted with an element of drama. Being positive, sincere and consistent are still vitally important.

One recipe for quality communication is to remember that the coach should:

- Know his/her stuff
- Be aware that the information to be communicated needs to be interesting
- Be aware of the complexity of the language used. (See below *)
- Be aware that the voice is more effective in communication when it changes in pitch and volume in order to emphasise points
- Be aware that the pace of delivery can indicate urgency or plenty of time
- Be aware that questions ensure that the group are actively involved
- Be aware that facial expressions and eye contact maintains interest
- Be aware that gestures (especially the hands) and body language in general are powerful communicating tools
- Be aware that spatial awareness can lead to good contact, i.e., the communicator moves around in order to enter different peoples personal space
- Be aware of the body language of the group and pick up the signs when a change is needed (See more in the section "Communication between Coach and Captain" below.)
- Be aware of how to recognise boredom or lack of interest in a group
- Be aware that how he/she looks is important to the listener, i.e., clothes and appearance
- Be aware that the most important skill a coach needs is the judgement as to what to say and what not to say about a particular issue.

* Know the players in the team. Avoid language that is too complex and may not be understood. A rough guide is that the reading age of a tabloid newspaper is significantly lower than the reading age of a broadsheet newspaper. Make your language accessible by choosing words that seem appropriate to a particular group of players. Alternatively, if a complex word is used, then, following the complex word, offer alternative words for those players who might not otherwise understand.

I mentioned earlier that it was sometimes difficult to distinguish between the coach and the individual and the coach and the team. Because of its dramatic importance to the National Club Championship win in 1999 I recount the details of communication that took place during the last 16 match between Wolverhampton and Farnworth when Wolverhampton, who were at home in front of their own supporters, were 27 for 5 chasing 164 to win!

This was a **team** chase that was handled in a coach/individual way. The communication was slanted to suit the individuals concerned, but the essential communication revolved around the following strategy. It was a mixture of questions and comments and what follows is paraphrased and not the actual words that were spoken.

- What do you think of the bowling attack we have seen?
- Are we in this position because of the quality of Farnworth's bowling or the lack of quality of our own batting?
- What run rate do we need to score at in order to win the match?
- Do we need to score at that rate now or is it better to build steadily now and save any risks for later?
- Will that require high or low risk?
- Which bowler appears to be the most dangerous?
- How many overs does that bowler have left?
- Do you think the remaining bowlers, based on evidence, are going to give you a ball or two per over that you can score off?
- Have you identified the weaker bowlers?
- Which fielders look suspect?
- What do you think is needed?
- What style of cricket is required?
- What agreed team qualities will we have to show today?

With some players this required more questions and a prompting approach to steer the players into finding the appropriate answers. In others, all of the above questions were not required, but by asking questions, the players had to go through a thinking process. If, as coach, I had just told them what to do, in the heat of the situation they may not have heard me. My job was to keep them calm and focussed and very clear as to how they were going to approach the task. The calmness comes through having an understanding of what it is you are trying to achieve and having a strategy to achieve it. Sitting quietly next to the next batter can also transmit calm.

From 27 for 5 the scores went:

54 for 6 ➤ 108 for 7 ➤ 118 for 8 ➤ 164 for 8

Players batted according to the situation, played within their limitations, played at the appropriate risk levels and thrived in the challenge of battle, and deservedly won a game.

This questioning style, structured to suit each individual player, can be a very powerful tool for the coach to employ when considering what style of communication is appropriate for his/her players and team. The ECB Level III course covers this area of "Coaching Style and Maturity".

The "Coaching Style" helps coaches to look at their communication in terms of concern for people or concern for task, and helps them understand the numerous ways in which decisions can be arrived at. It also helps the coach to identify their own behaviour in terms of their preferred way of working - words like training and instruction, prescription, telling on the one hand and facilitating, consulting, and empowering on the other. This helps coaches recognise that one method is not necessarily right but that a mixture of styles is perhaps desirable.

The concept of "Maturity" helps the coach decide what is required for a particular group of players. The general desire would be to help individual/pairs/groups within the team to become more mature and to take increasingly greater responsibility for their own actions. The coach may have to prescribe or tell with immature teams and when a team is underachieving. I believe that the coach should always be looking for ways to make the team increasingly self-sufficient. The end of chapter 6 says more about this issue.

Another example of a team issue that can be handled in a coach/individual way, which contrasts totally from the one described above relates to crucial communication and the team before a match. The circumstances were real. The team had been selected for the weekend and the bowlers knew their roles. On the Thursday, a key bowler was injured. All the bowlers were telephoned to explain the situation and to talk about the adjustments that they would need to make to their role for the Saturday match. This also included a telephone call to a batter who bowled occasionally to say that they could be called upon. This sort of communication enables players to mentally prepare in the appropriate manner. The same practice would be applied if a batter became indisposed for whatever reason after selection.

This telephone system wasn't difficult to operate because Friday telephone calls to all players were routine.

COMMUNICATION BETWEEN THE COACH AND THE CAPTAIN

This is a very important component of team success. The communication that any relationship needs to succeed is crucial and in a cricket context it is especially the case when it comes to the relationship between coach and captain.

In using the word captain, I would like the reader to include the vice-captain, as a group of three is often more effective than two. It spreads the load and the directions in which players can be influenced. Occasionally a meeting between the coach and captain might include captain, vice-captain, senior player(s) and coach. So the use of the word captain, although frequently one-to-one, should be interpreted flexibly.

The diagram at the beginning of this chapter clearly indicated the importance that was placed on the communication between coach and captain. Both are bound to be more effective if they are "singing from the same hymn sheet". This can only be achieved through spending time together. Shared strategic vision means that coach and captain can work from different standpoints to affect the collective attitudes of the team.

The same three phases described earlier are relevant in this area:

- Winter leading to pre-season
- Practice
- Match play

Winter leading to pre-season and the captain

This is the most important period. Groundwork done here pays handsome dividends.

In order to prevent repetition, there are numerous examples that need to be cited here for the reader to consult.

Chapter 2 - "Preparation" - 'The Heart of Success'

- The mid March or earlier meeting between coach and captain
- The follow-up meeting with captain and vice-captain if the vice-captain wasn't involved in the first meeting
- The pre-season consultation meeting with players at which the captain played an important part

Chapter 5 - "Match Action" - 'Making Things Happen'

- The post season meeting to "Exorcise the ghost" of the 2000 season of underachievement, again at which the captain played an important part
- The agenda for the meeting with captain and vice-captain (detailed on page 170)

During a spell with a club, a coach may have to work with more than one captain. In this case the process of building up strong foundations has to start again. If however, the coach has established positive, quality relationships with the whole squad, then this makes it easier when, in a likely scenario, one of the squad moves up to take over as captain.

There are no magic formulas for establishing a quality relationship with the captain, but certainly mutual respect is vital, and a willingness to stay open-minded and flexible. If the captain is new, then extra discussion time needs to be found to decide how captain and coach are going to work during the season. They will need to address the following questions: 'How often do we need to meet? What will be the focus of our communications? What roles and responsibilities are we each going to take? Will there be overlap? If so...

Many of the points listed earlier when dealing with a team can transfer to a relationship with the captain and a discussion that revolves around "Communication" - 'The Crucial Factor' is time well spent. I think it important, for example, for the coach to share with the captain the thoughts he or she has as to how to identify the state of mind of the team, so that both can be on the lookout for the tell-tail signs. (Towards the end of Chapter 5, there is a diagram that indicates the sort of symptoms that identify when a team are on track, improving or in decline, and that is followed by a list of 16 suggested ways of "picking up the vibes".) A few symptoms, to give a flavour, include: "On track" - players listen to each other, cricket is the focus, culture of praise, enjoyment, "Improving" - responsibility accepted, open discussion, constructive dialogue, "Decline" - criticism, missed practice, advice ignored, arguments. The full list involves 30 symptoms.

In my experience, the captain is happy for the coach to take the lead in a discussion. The coach should therefore create an agenda which highlights a suggested approach, but which leaves what is discussed open to revision. It is merely a structure that provides coat-pegs on which to hang opinions. The main thing is to get the captain talking, not listening to the coach! It is he/she who will be making the all-important decisions on the day and therefore strategy has to be clear. The alternative to suggesting an approach is to compile a list of questions for the captain to consider. An example of this was highlighted in chapter 3 in the short 'tactical' section 'Captain and tactics'.

If the captain and coach share the same enthusiasm for the way they want the team to play, then the job of the coach is made much easier. If on the other hand the captain is at variance with the coach, then there is a fundamental decision to be made. If it were a professional team, then the coach could well have the last word off the field of play, but the coach cannot control events when the team are on the field except to a limited degree. The same would apply with an age group county side, but when it comes to an amateur top club side, it is less easy for the coach to have the last word. He/she needs to strive for agreement.

Part of the success of 1998 and 1999 when the team were well led by the captain is that my attitude as coach was to work around the decisions of the captain and to support them whatever was decided. By and large, we were on the same track. The differences were relatively small because the side were very successful and 'catching the fish that slipped through the net' a manageable task. I believe, in any case, that a captain who makes a tactical error but carries through their decision with conviction can often make it work.

When things went wrong in the 2000 season, this approach wasn't enough. The differences in opinion over selection or tactics were more significant and more difficult to compensate for. However, the experience has taught me that when things are stuttering, then more time must be spent in discussion with the captain.

Practice and the captain

As with meetings, the captain is generally happy to let the coach get on with organising a practice. The main thing is for the coach to communicate what he/she is doing with the team and why. If the captain understands where the coach is coming from, then he/she will be in a better position to support.

I believe that the captain and senior players need to take responsibility in practice. So a well-constructed programme will enable this to happen. Chapter 2 refers to how a practice session is organised and there is plenty of opportunity to involve the captain and senior players.

One advantage of practice is that it is a fixed day of the week, when discussion is possible between captain and coach. The day of the practice is important and for three years Monday, which was really too close to the weekend, has been chosen to make it convenient for selection purposes. At the instigation of the new captain however, this has been moved to Thursday evening. This should be much better as it separates selection from practice. There are several advantages in using a Thursday for practice:

- "Baggage" from the weekend will have reduced in intensity
- Players will be fresher
- The practice can be focussed towards the weekend ahead rather than be reflective on the weekend that's past.
- The coach will have had time to research the previous weekend results and scorecards and have prepared a proposed strategy for the forthcoming game

- The coach and captain will have time to routinely discuss these proposals
- It provides a more logical structure to communication channels

From the coach/captain point of view, it above all, makes communication easier, as it allows the preparation for the next match to be more professional and strategically planned. Time to talk is always a limitation otherwise.

Match play and the captain

The preparation during the week should make match days easier for both the captain and coach. Match days should become more a case of fine-tuning the tactics to suit conditions and any late fitness news about our own side and/or the opposition.

With a plan for the game agreed, the contact between coach and captain doesn't have to be frequent, although the coach will have more contact with the captain than with any other player. Each can get on with their task of motivating the team in the knowledge that they are on the same wavelength.

Once the game plan has been decided, the main function of the coach in the communication with the captain is to be available whenever the captain wishes to discuss anything and to present ideas for the captain to feed on which could influence the result of the game. Agreed tactics is always the desired outcome.

It may not appear much as this section is quite small, but time spent in communication with the captain, which clarifies policies and tactics is essential if the team are to be well led and motivated.

Final thought for this chapter

The coach has the task of seeing the "bigger picture" and of deciding how to coordinate all the various strands of communication. Every coach is unique, and so, although there have been many suggested approaches, the coach must remain true to themselves.

One analogy would be to regard all coaches as having the same road map, even though aiming for different destinations. What's more, even when the destination is common, there are 100's and 100's of different routes. Over time as we become familiar with the main routes to a destination, we discover short cuts. In the same way as a friend may introduce a quicker or more effective route along roads that we didn't at one time even know existed, so a coach will discover better ways of communicating. This book and this chapter have hopefully introduced you to a number of new roads.

MATCH ACTION : MAKING THINGS HAPPEN

The introduction to chapter 6 "THE COACH - Rising to the Challenge" helps to put into context the specific preparation that follows in this chapter. It explains how I started coaching a premier league cricket club.

There are three different situations described in this chapter:

1 – Making things happen in league matches when the team are generally successful.
(The Birmingham and District Premier Cricket League 1998)

2 – Making things happen in a sudden death knock-out competition
(The ECB National Club Championship 1999)

3 – Trying to make things happen in league matches when the team are unsuccessful.
(The Birmingham and District Premier Cricket League 2000)

1 – So how did we prepare to make things happen in league matches during 1998 when the team were very successful?

PRE-SEASON MEETING AND PRE-SEASON PRACTICE

The preparation described in chapter 2 was not possible due to the timing of the appointment as coach. Some of the players were known but a significant number were not.

Preparation was therefore not ideal. In order to cut a few corners, I followed the pattern below. It might provide a starting point for a newly appointed coach.

a. Obtain reports to the Annual General Meeting of the chairman and captain or club captain for the previous season and any available before that. This gives an overview of the club, and an indication of the way the club thinks - the direction in which it is going.

b. Attend any winter nets or pre-season planned events if possible and, if the timing of the appointment gives you time:

c. Arrange a meeting with the captain or the captain and vice-captain, if that is more appropriate, to establish agreed objectives for the season.

d. Agree a list of players who are considered to be probable/possible 1st team material. Categorise them according to what they offer: batter, bowler, all-rounder, wicket keeper, etc.

e. Arrange a pre-season meeting of players at which the captain and the coach can outline their vision of the future and invite players to express their views about it. (Please note that in subsequent years, the players, I believe, should be more actively involved in setting the agenda for the season.) A detailed pre-season meeting can be found in chapter 2 together with a full pre-season schedule that I have used when there was time to plan well ahead.

f. Specific to the 1998 season was the overhead projection of an acetate sheet, which explained how the Birmingham & District Premier League had been set up and how it related to the feeder leagues in 1998 and subsequent seasons.

g. Specific to this season was an explanation of the playing regulations and in particular the points scoring system. It is surprising how many players drift into a season without this sort of information.

h. Agree the practice night and times and give some idea as to how you would like to organise it and something of your expectations.

i. As soon as the overseas player arrives, arrange a meeting to establish the way that you are going to work together, where this is appropriate to your situation. This was vital and led to a great deal of support throughout the season. He brought a professional approach and culture to the club that supported the values that I wanted to establish in our team. It is also important to recognise that the professional/overseas player needs a different style of relationship.

PRE-MATCH PREPARATION

We targeted a time whereby the warm up started 1 hour before the scheduled time for the match to start. In practice this most often became nearer to 45 minutes by the time everyone was ready. Cajoling rather than getting annoyed became the preferred way of getting the show on the road.

I would arrive ready changed and, while the players were getting ready, place plastic mini cones in the form of a rectangular grid and, separately, erect kwik cricket stumps at the end of a square or just off the square for bowling practice at the end of the warm up.

The warm up was made up of several components. General warm up, stretches, catching and fielding ball skills involving nine of the team before players opted for what they needed, be this bowling at kwik cricket stumps, throw-downs for batters or close/medium/high catching. The reason for it being only 9 players for the warm-up is explained in the early part of chapter 6. It reflects on the flexibility needed of a coach when the ideal proves impossible with a particular group of players who represent a cross-section of amateur players who work during the week and sometimes Saturday mornings.

See end of the chapter for an example of a typical warm up. One of the key issues is that there must be, in my opinion, the element of routine. This becomes very important in the big games, and will be mentioned again in the preparation for the National Club Knock Out final at Lords.

We finished with a team talk before the players were given the last 15 minutes to prepare in their own way. This tried to recognise the individuality of each player. Some liked peace and quiet and would find their own private space, others found it absolutely necessary to engage in conversation while others liked to listen to music on their headphones.

So what was the team talk about?

Two newspapers, the "Sunday Mercury" and the Monday edition of the "Birmingham Post" publish the scorecards of the weekend matches in the Birmingham and District Premier League. That was the starting point.

I would also look in the local "Express & Star" at the weekly league roundup, and note any other bits of "gossip". "Gossip" is an important part of information gathering irrespective of whether this is from a newspaper or word of mouth.

I would spend about an hour per week updating information from all clubs such that when we played them, there was a record of their form so far in the season, and more particularly their form over the last five matches.

The following is the process that I went through each week after first creating a single A4 sheet for each team in the league including Wolverhampton:

- Cut out the scorecards and the league table and pritt stick them onto a piece of A4 paper
- Photocopy them twice
- Cut out each scorecard (one for each team involved)
- Number the match round e.g. 6th match and indicate whether it was home or away for each team
- Stick a scorecard onto the A4 sheet of both relevant clubs
- Stripe in coloured highlighter pen where the match was played, the result of the match and the points allocated.

See next page for an example of an opposition scorecard record for a league team.

Having updated the records of all clubs, I would then concentrate on the preparation for the next match. A form was used to collect together the relevant information and this became the basis of the pre-match talk.

Questions asked? Mainly of the opposition, but also ourselves!

- What's the sequence of results in the last five matches?
- How typical is it of their overall playing record?
- Where were the games played?

WALSALL (98)

① (A)   ② (H)   ③ (A)

WB Dartmouth v Walsall

Walsall

Jenkinson b Parsons		60
Baker run out		33
Clarke st Swainson b Sajjad		78
Mills c Rawnsley b Shah		55
Perry not out		2
Watson not out		3
Extras		22
Total: (4 wkts, 55 overs)		263

Bowling: Sajjad 16-3-51-1; Shah 13-e-71-1; Dalton 5-1-39-0; Rawnsley 13-4-46-0; Parsons 8-1 10-1

WB Dartmouth

Waterhouse c Patel b Arnold		47
Mohammad run out		18
Zahoor c Shipp b Patel		7
Dalton lbw Arnold		1
Sajjad c Shipp b Arnold		9
Rawnsley b Arnold		0
Hollyhead st Shipp b Patel		1
Cox c Shipp b Watson		6
Shah b Mayer		15
Swainson not out		9
Parsons not out		6
Extras		16
Total: (9 wkts) 55 overs		133

Bowling: Arnold 23-14-4-34; Watson 13-2-1-58; Mayer 11-5-1-27; Patel 8-5-2-9.
Result: Winning draw Walsall (6 pts). WB Dartmouth (2 pts).

Walsall v Stratford

Walsall

Archer c O'Connell b Troughton		60
Baker c Wootton b Troughton		64
Clarke c Halsaz b Troughton		4
Mills st Ferguson b O'Connell		2
Perry c Humphrey b Troughton		24
Watson c Kerby b O'Connell		38
Patel c Humphrey b Troughton		12
Lewis b O'Connell		5
Dalton not out		0
Arnold c Howells b Troughton		24
Mayer not out		5
Extras		11
Total: (9wkts, 55 overs)		222

Bowling: Kerby 6-0-39-0; Palmer 6-0-25-0; Halsaz 6-0-36-0; O'Connell 13-3-60-3; Troughton 15-1-47-6

Stratford

Halsaz lbw b Arnold		32
Wootton run out		0
Graham c Dalton b Mayer		11
Howells c Mills b Arnold		10
Humphrey c Dalton b Mayer		10
Troughton c Dalton b Arnold		32
Pigeon c Clarke b Lewis		9
Kerby c Patel b Arnold		37
O'Connell not out		20
Palmer not out		0
Extras		12
Total: (8 wkts 54.3 overs)		224

Bowling: Arnold 27.3-5-89-4 Watson 4-0-24-0; Mayer 15-6-56-2. Lewis 6-1-47-1
Result: Stratford (10 pts) won by 2 wkts.

Coventry & NW v Walsall

Coventry & NW

Powell c Dalton b Arnold		0
Hughes c Clarke b Arnold		21
Bell c Dalton b Watson		0
Roberts c Clarke b Watson		4
Platt b Mayer		15
Pathan lbw Arnold		0
Patel run out		8
Preece lbw Arnold		24
Young not out		5
Mwangwall c Clarke b Arnold		0
Taplin lbw Watson		11
Extras		3
Total		91

Bowling: Arnold 25-10-34-5; Watson 12-1-31-3; Mayer 13-6-18-1.

Walsall

Archer not out		34
Baker c Powell b Bell		50
Clarke not out		0
Extras		6
Total: (1 Wkt, 30 overs)		93

Bowling: Meanham 7-1-10-0 Young 0-1-20-1; Powell 4-1-10-0, Preece 7-0-33-0; Taplin 5-1-12-0; Bell 1-0-5-1.
Result: Walsall (14 pts) won by 9 wkts.

Walsall v Barnt Green

Barnt Green

Hudson b Arnold
Martin c Clarke b Watson
Froggatt lbw b Arnold
Ellis b Mayer
Viljoen b Mayer
Patel c Dhillon b Arnold
Galloway c Mayer b Arnold
Hall not out
Mackay b Mayer
Oxley b Arnold
Anderson not out
Extras

Total (9wkts 42 overs)
Bowling: Arnold 21-3-72-5; Watson 9-0-3
Mayer 12-2-39-3   Walsall

Dean lbw MacKay
Baker lbw Pate
Clarke c Anderson b MacKay
Mills c & b Viljoen
Perry not out
Watson lbw Patel
Patel (K) not out
Extras

Total (5 wkts 28.2 overs)
Bowling: MacKay 6-1-54-2; Ellis 5-0-36-0
G Viljoen 5-0-35-1; Hudson 7.1-0-22-0.
Pate 3-1-6-2
Result: Walsall (10 pts) won by 5 wickets

OLD HILL v WALSALL
Old Hill

J Robinson c Lewis b Mayer .....38￼
J Wright c Archer b Arnold .....11￼
K Hamilton lbw b Watson .....1￼
D Banks lbw Arnold .....10￼
A Heidrich c Perry b Mayer .....8￼
K Pearson b Mayer .....1￼
L Caldicott lbw Mayer .....0￼
D Manning c Dhillon b Arnold .....17￼
D Williams lbw Mayer .....3￼
N DeSilva c Dhillon b Arnold .....1￼
P Lyman not out .....0￼
Extras .....--

Total 103
Bowling: K Arnold 20.1-6-45-4, A Watson
10-1-30-1, J Mayer 10-2-21-5

Walsall

S Dean c Robinson b Hamilton .....26￼
P Baker not out .....42￼
N Archer not out .....34￼
Extras 2

Total (one wicket) 104
Bowling: K Hamilton 8-1-54-1, A Heidrich 9-2-23-0, G Williams 7-1-17-0, P Lyman 4.5-1-10-0.
Walsall won by nine wickets.

Walsall v Aston Unity
Aston Unity

Neal c Dhillon .....8￼
Hussain c Dhillon b Arnold .....7￼
Hughes c Dean b Watson .....0￼
Chagger c Dhillon b Arnold .....9￼
Cresswell c Baker b Lewis .....55￼
Dave (D) c Clarke b Arnold .....3￼
Ellis c Mills b Arnold .....3￼
Newton c Dean b Mayer .....9￼
Bradley lbw Mayer .....6￼
Veness not out .....16￼
Dave (P) b Mayer .....0￼
Extras 3

Total 43 overs 124
Bowling: Arnold 13-0-40-5 Watson 9-2-39-1.
Mayer 12-3-28-3, Lewis 3-0-15-1.
Walsall

Dean c&b Creswell .....47￼
Baker not out .....47￼
Clarke not out .....24￼
Extras 6

Total (1 wkt, 22.1 overs) 127
Bowling: Veness 5-0-37-0; Newton 5-0-30-0;
Brasley 5-0-19-0; Creswell 6-1-27-1; Hughes
1.1-0-6-0.
Result: Walsall (14 pts) won by 9 wickets.

Walsall v Kidderminster

Walsall

Archer b Chapman	12
Baker c Gault b Chapman	0
Clarke b Hayes	28
Mills c Scofield b Hemming	50
Perry c Scofield b Hemming	11
Watson c Tidmarsh b Hemming	20
Patel c Chapman b Hemming	24
Lewis c Hemming b Mansell	4
Arnold c Mansell b Hemming	17
Dhillon st Vinas b Mansell	1
Mayer not out	4
Extras	15

Total: (47.3 overs) 181
Bowling: Chapman 8-2-32-2; Scofield 11-0-44-0; Hayes 11-2-41-1; Hemming 12-3-34-5; Mansell 10-1-34-2

Kidderminster

Mansell c Dhillon b Watson	10
Williamson c Baker b Watson	10
Scofield b Watson	9
Ralph c Perry b Mayer	2
Tidmarsh c Perry b Arnold	1
Columball lbw b Arnold	1
Chapman lbw b Arnold	0
Vinas c Dhillon b Arnold	6
Gault not out	0
Hayes lbw b Arnold	1
Hemming c Mayer b Arnold	6
Extras	

Total: (34.3 overs) 73
Bowling: Arnold 17.3-6-27-6; Watson 11-1-28-3; Mayer 6-2-11
Result: Walsall (14 pts) won by 108 runs.

Wolverhampton v Walsall

Walsall

Dean b Franklin	15
Baker b Franklin	
Clarke b Heap	
Perry c Mackelworth b Franklin	14
Watson c Mackelworth b Franklin	17
Archer not out	
Patel c Henderson b Heap	3
Lewis c Williams b Heap	4
Arnold b Franklin	0
Dhillon run out	1
Extras	6

Total: (9 wkts, 28 overs) 68
Bowling: Franklin 14-2-35-5; Perry 7-1-0-5-0; Heap 11-0-24-3

Wolverhampton

Lampitt c Patel b Mayer	25
Henderson not out	36
Franklin not out	4
Extras	2

Total: (1 wkt, 22.3 overs) 69
Bowling: Lewis 4-0-23-0; Arnold 11-3-22-0; Patel 5-1-13-0; Mayer 4.3-0-9-1
Result: Wolverhampton (10 pts) won by 9 wkts

Stourbridge v Walsall

Walsall

Dean c Boroughs b Francis	85
Baker run out	7
Clarke c Boroughs b Francis	29
Mills c Boroughs b Francis	2
Perry c Adehead b Francis	5
Watson lbw b Boroughs	9
Archer not out	21
Patel b Boroughs	19
Arnold not out	2
Extras	25

Total: (7 wkts, 43 overs) 164
Bowling: Johnson 15-1-59-0; Boroughs 10-0-51-2; Francis 18-1-64-4

Stourbridge

Boroughs c Patel b Arnold	48
Adehead c Patel b Arnold	12
Price c Dhillon b Arnold	19
Davenport c Patel b Arnold	25
Johnson b Mayer	6
Round st Dhillon b Arnold	4
Talley not out	0
Francis c Patel b Arnold	0
Tandy lbw b Arnold	16
Extras	

Total: (8 wkts, 43 overs) 131
Bowling: Arnold 22-8-43-7; Watson 5-1-22-0; Mayer 16-5-54-1
Result: Winning draw. Walsall (6 pts), Stourbridge (2 pts)

Walsall v Smethwick

Walsall

Dean c Binks b Simms 13
Baker c Binks b Simms 10
Clarke c Binks b Simms 8
Mills c McDonald b Folkes 17
Perry c Moore b Folkes 20
Watson st Binks b Javaid 21
Archer c Binks b Javaid 1
Patel c Akhlaq b Javaid 0
Arnold not out 18
Dhillon not out 10
Extras 2

Total (8 wkts, 42 overs) 120

Bowling: Simms 12-4-29-3, Khan 10-2-26-0; Folkes 10-2-30-2; Javaid 10-4-28-3.

Smethwick

Ross lbw b Arnold 4
Scragg c Clarke b Watson 11
Akhlaq c Clarke b Arnold 4
McDonald not out 50
Patel lbw b Arnold 0
Moore lbw b Arnold 0
Extras 12

Total (5 wkts, 39.1 overs) 130

Bowling: Arnold 20-8-53-4; Watson 8-0-34-1; Mayor 13.1-4-34-0.
Result: Smethwick (10 pts) won by 5 wkts.
* All other matches were abandoned because of rain with each team involved receiving 2 pts.

Moseley v Walsall

Walsall

Archer (N) c Eustace (S) b Pretorius 10
Baker st Eustace (S) b Eustace (M) 62
Clarke c Ostler b Eustace (M) 63
Mills c Stokes b Stephenson 15
Archer (R) b Stephenson 5
Perry not out 16
Watson c Eustace (S) b Eustace (M) 1
Patel c Webster b Eustace (M) 1
Wicker not out 9
Extras 10

Total (7 wkts, 55 overs) 192

Bowling: Pretorius 11-0-36-1; Webster 10-1-24-0; Stephenson 17-2-63-2; Eustace (N) 17-1-65-4.

Moseley

Stokes c Mills b Mayor 11
Westwood b Wicker 32
Frost lbw Watson 65
Ostler c Wicker b Watson 34
Botton not out 16
Trishu b Watson 0
Webster lbw Patel 0
Eustace not out 20
Extras 18

Total (6wkts, 53.1 overs) 196

Bowling: Watson 19-2-71-3, Mayor 19-3-46-1; Wicker 5-0-18-0; Patel 10.1-0-49-1.
Result: Moseley (10 pts) won by 4 wkts.

The information tracked.

- How many runs were scored on which pitch and how many wickets taken?
- How did it compare with the opposition performance?
- Who scored the runs?
- How did their key batters perform?
- What batting order was used? Stable/unstable
- Who took the wickets?
- How did their key bowlers perform? Set pattern?

DATE ....OPPONENTS ....

OVERALL COMMENT ....

KEY OPPOSITION TARGETS ....

POSITION IN TABLE....P   W   Wd   Ld   L   Aban   Bon   Pts

Overall Record ....

Last five matches ....

AGAINST &
RESULT......1..............2.............3.............4.............5..............

SCORES..

BATTING

1...

2...

3...

4...

5...

6 ....

Comments rate/aver ....

BOWLING

1 ....

2 ....

3 ....

4 ....

5 ....

6 ....

Comments str.rate/econ/aver ....

....

The form above recorded the relevant information. It is reduced here for illustrative purposes, but is normally A4 size. A larger version that can be photocopied and/or adapted is included at the end of chapter two. The column for wins, defeats, draws, bonus points etc. would need to be customised for a particular set of playing conditions.

Examples of the sort of information gleaned from newspapers, from gossip and from previous knowledge about the opposition and their players would be shaped ready for the team talk along the following lines. The example is taken from 1998:

Opponents:	Walsall
Overall Comment:	5 consecutive wins in the last 5 matches - they are ready for a "bump"! Walsall 72 points plays Wolverhampton 51 points so this is a double pointer.
	Walsall lost at Wolverhampton in 1997 160+ plays 130+ so they won't be relishing playing here.
	Conditions are wet so they would probably be happy with an abandoned game. Big question - will they be up for it?
Key opposition targets	Player "A" is always potentially dangerous - plays well in the V and likes to hit the ball. (Right handed) Player "B" is the man in form. Except for a duck in the last match, he's put together 6 good scores on the bounce. (Left handed)
	Both are more vulnerable against spin.
	(Discussions had been going on for 2 weeks with the captain whom I had tried to persuade to open the bowling with spin.)
	I'd then go through other batters. E.g., Player "C" has also been in form, but there is doubt as to whether he is playing.
	Player "D" is their main strike bowler. He bowls straight, usually throughout, but he's not a world-beater. It's time he had a poor game. Strike rate 4.66 overs per wicket at an average of 8.97 but we must be positive against him. Look for singles.

I'd then go through support bowlers and then finish with a final comment like: They've got everything to lose while we've got everything to gain. Let's try and match our early season fielding performance against Stratford. Let's go for it - be mentally positive.

Result: Walsall 68 for 9 declared in a 25 over match, Wolverhampton 69 for 1. (Note: 10 points to Wolverhampton. Would have been 14 had Walsall not declared.) The conditions were difficult for batters.

This was a crucial win at an important stage of the season. It was a vital springboard for team confidence. Detailed preparation had a lot to do with this result.

Another example of detailed planning came at the end of the 1998 season when Wolverhampton entered the last match with a lead of 7 points.

Wolverhampton 157 points   Walsall 150 points

Points system in the league at the time:

Bowl opposition out in win	14 points
Win without bowling opposition out	10 points
Tie	5 points
Winning draw	6 points
Losing draw	2 points
Abandoned	2 points

The winning draw was usually achieved when batting first and the losing draw when batting second except in rain affected matches when run-rate was the criteria. The chart below shows that out of 25 possible results, 20 would result in Wolverhampton winning the league.

W O L V E R H A M P T O N					
W Points	0	2	6	10	14
A 0	W	W	W	W	W
L 2	W	W	W	W	W
S 6	W	W	W	W	W
A 10	L	L	W	W	W
L 14	L	L	L	W	W

(Left vertical label: W A L S A L L)

The above chart was shown to the players. We agreed that if we got 0 or 2 points, we didn't deserve to win the title.

"The only result where we can play well and not win the title is to get a winning draw (6 points) while Walsall get a 14-point win."

In the event, we lost the toss, were put into bat and so had to go for the win. There was mobile 'phone contact with the other match involving Walsall, but the players were not told what was going on. They were going to win the title through what *they* did, not what Walsall didn't do!

Results: Wolverhampton 14 point win and the title.
                Walsall 2 points in an abandoned game and
                second place.

Included in the preparation for this game was a detailed weather forecast. If the Walsall game had not been abandoned the information could have proved crucial.

The forecast was "Vigorous depression moving south. A.M. bright early leading to cloud and showers (some heavy). Bright late morning. P.M. good sunny spells, a few showers, some sharp." It looked as if it was going to be the luck of the draw. It was enough to indicate that there could be interruptions and therefore it would be worth calculating the possible effects of losing time.

For example, assuming a finishing time of 8.20p.m. the latest the match could start was 5.10p.m. In such circumstances the game would be 25 overs per side. There were detailed scenarios worked out for different situations but the point being made is that league regulations, in circumstances of unpredictable weather conditions, can be a useful source of tactical inspiration! Two telephone numbers for up-to-date weather forecasts were also taken to the game in order to retain the opportunity for assessing changes to predicted weather and thereby maintain tactical flexibility. In the normal course of a season, teams are generally more philosophical about weather, but this amount of detail appeared justified to me as it was the last match and the league title was at stake.

Feedback to players - individual

While preparation as outlined is considered to be the heart of success, players make little progress in their own performance unless there is feedback. Some players have the ability to be objective about their own performance and can adjust their game accordingly, while others (most) benefit from the feedback and objectivity of the coach.

Positive feedback to players can be seen as part of preparation for the next performance.

It is the coach's job to observe players in both practice and match situations and to analyse their performance. This will include observation and analysis before, during and after the performance. Having analysed the performance, the analysis has to be evaluated before it can form the substance of feedback to the individual. The evaluation requires expert interpretation of what was observed and analysed as it forms the basis of the coach's decision as to what type of feedback/comment/discussion is appropriate for a particular player. The quality of interpretation and the subsequent feedback that is given is probably the most decisive factor that distinguishes the quality coach from the average at top club level. There is choice in how feedback is managed as discussed in chapter 4.

The feedback relates to the five "Vital Ingredients" found in chapter 3 - "Integration - mental, physical, technical, tactical and lifestyle", although any particular feedback is more likely to concentrate on the mental, technical and tactical.

The evaluation of the observed and analysed performance and the subsequent feedback leads to a planned approach towards the player's development. At top club level this becomes a development route agreed between player and coach. More was said about this in chapter 4 in the section on the coach and the individual player. The ECB Level II course deals with the analysis of performance. While one of the key aspects that the course deals with is the analysis of technique, it also introduces the analysis of tactics, behaviour and emotions, fitness, diet, health, injury status and coaching effectiveness. The ECB Level III course on the other hand has a significant component that develops the coach's skill in communication.

Feedback to individual players can sometimes be carried out on the day of the match but it is more likely to be discussed on a later occasion at say the next practice. It is better for it to be face-to-face, but sometimes it has to be on the 'phone. The coach needs to become an opportunist! Choosing the right time is important.

Feedback to players - team

Team feedback needs to be approached from a different angle. At top club level, the ideal situation would be for all players to attend practice and to be part of a feedback which acts as preparation for the next match. See chapter 2 - "Preparation" - A "Typical" Practice Session. This would give the team time to reflect on the team performance and to have recovered from any personal wounds.

The reality is that the chances of getting the whole of the league team together from the previous match are remote. Feedback immediately after the match is not difficult if it follows a polished performance. It can be a delicate matter, however, after a poor performance. The challenge for the coach in this situation is to decide how valuable feedback would be, and once committed to feedback, how to manage it. Not easy, but if the nettle isn't grasped in certain situations, perceptions of performance can quickly change by the time the match is "revisited"!

The important factor in the coach's decision as to how to manage the feedback if something constructive is to emerge is to decide how interactive he/she wants it to be. It is easy to deliver a judgement from on high and to download an opinion; far more difficult to manage an interactive discussion in which players are encouraged to contribute. Despite the difficulty, the development of such a management skill is one that the top club coach will need to acquire.

The **1999 season** started with a players meeting in April at which the following question was put to the players. This is the short version. The detailed version can be found in Chapter 2 in the section called "Example of a Pre-season Players' Meeting. April 1999".

"What have we got to do to replicate the success of 1998 season?"

Little did we know that we were going to win the National Club Championship at Lord's!

Players meeting agenda:

There was first a brief introduction, but rather than have a discussion with 15 players at the same time the following process was followed:

- The squad were asked to pair up and then brainstorm all the factors that they thought were significant in the success of 1998 and then to choose their best 5.

- After approximately 10 minutes discussion, each pair reported back to the whole group their top 5. All the points were listed on a flip chart. There were 17 different possibilities.

- Pairs were then asked to list their top 5 out of the 17 and a point was scored against each selection.

The outcome was a consensus as to what the players thought should be our top 5 priorities..

OUR AGREED PRIORITIES

TEAM SPIRIT – WORKING IN UNITS

PREPARATION – TRAINING / PRACTICE

MENTAL STRENGTH – (Toughness)

FOCUS – (Concentration)

ENJOYMENT

The evening was very successful and the priorities above were used on numerous occasions during the season.

There was one additional idea that I threw in as coach. I believe that the contact between players in squads/teams is very important. I showed the circle below and explained what I thought it represented. This is the same diagram as in chapter 2, but it bears repetition because it is so important.

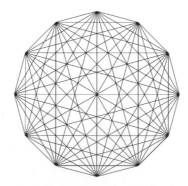

- Essentially in any one game, there are 11 players and the coach
- It is the responsibility of each and every person to establish contact with each of the others in the team and to establish, at least, "working" relationships.

- The bonding that this develops is the core of team spirit
- It is the inter-connections that hold the team together in times of crisis.

This was the background to the 1999 season in what was to lead to success in the ECB National Club Championship.

2 – So how did we prepare to make things happen in the National Knockout in 1999?

Starting with the Regional Final

The key difference between league and knockout games is that in knockout games, the opposition is frequently of an unknown quantity and, in the case of away games, the ground and pitch is of an unknown quantity.

Alsager (Away)   **A team from South Cheshire**

Tasks: **The opposition ground**

- Where is it? Clear directions for travel purposes.
- Visit the ground close enough to the match to get an idea of which pitch has been prepared.
- How wet/dry is the square and outfield?
- How green is the square and outfield?
- Note the slopes - end to end and sideways
- Pace out the boundaries behind bowlers wicket
- Pace out the sideways boundaries from edge of square
- Pace out the width of the square
- Look at wear patterns from previous matches

The opposition

- Make use of local contacts, e.g. my father lived 2 miles from ground
- Read local "free" newspapers who frequently give a full build up to the match and write about recent form and successful performances.
- Contact friends in the area (I used to play in the North Staffs & South Cheshire League in my youth) to establish how the wicket normally plays. e.g. slow and low

Result	Alsager 133 all out	Wolverhampton 137 for 4

A tighter game than it looks

Preparation

The vital research was to establish how the wicket normally played (slow and low) and to establish what sort of scores were "par for the course". It was a wicket where the opposition batters were going to be asked to do the work. Tactically, when bowling, it would be important that we didn't "hit the bat". This, together with ground dimensions, helped to ensure that bowlers bowled from the right ends, that the short boundary was protected and the long boundary defended by stopping two's.

The virtue we needed above all was patience.

Travelling in convoy help for a trouble free journey in the build up to the game.

Last 16

Farnworth (Home)   **A team from the Bolton area**

Tasks: **The opposition**

Make use of friends, e.g., Former Wolverhampton player recently moved into the Bolton area.

Ask about which league they play in, about recent performances and about key players and how they contribute.

Result: Farnworth 163 for 7   Wolverhampton 164 for 8

"Put to the sword" – the sort of game you have to win if you are to win the competition. At one stage 27 for 5! It could be argued that this was the most outstanding victory of the competition.

Preparation:

Preparation on reflection was perhaps a bit thin. It was not easy to get "chapter and verse". Knowledge of the importance of their professional and a reported lack in depth in both batting and bowling was vital to self-belief.

The virtues we had to show were "bottle", "determination" and "self belief". This was not something we had prepared for but something we had to respond to as the game evolved. 54 for 6, 108 for 7, 118 for 8.

How this was managed and communicated at the time comes in chapter 4 in the section "Match play and the team". It revolved around one-to-one discussion with batters before they went to the crease.

Last 8

Loughborough (Away)

Tasks:	**The opposition ground**

- The same considerations as for Alsager
- Clear directions to the ground required.
- Visit the ground close to the match and note the very green square, and the long boundaries sideways

The opposition

- While visiting Loughborough, find a local newsagent and either get hold of the local "free" paper or buy the local paper which previews matches.
- Use the experience of members of the team who have played with/against Loughborough. Plenty of grapevine knowledge.

Result:	**W'hampton 166 all out** **L'borough 99 all out**
	This was an inspired performance. The research paid off.

Preparation:	Visit to the ground was vital. Whole square was very green which suggested that Loughborough were going to pit their bowlers against ours.

Length of boundaries helped decide who bowled from which end.

The information in the "free" newspaper proved vital as we were prepared for the opening bats to "launch an opening attack". 28 for no wicket off 4 overs reduced to 56 for 6 off 20 overs.

The psychology of our preparation was becoming more and more important. We were a young team and needed to be mentally right.

The team talk included important virtues that we would need: patience, determination, self-control and self-belief.

Travelling in a luxury team coach ensured a relaxed and trouble free journey with plenty of opportunity for one-to-one discussion.

Semi-final

Harrogate (Home)

Tasks:

The opposition

- An experienced member of the team discovered that it was possible to obtain fax copies from the ECB of all of Harrogate's match scorecards.

- This enabled a full analysis to be undertaken in the same way as was routinely done for Birmingham and District Premier League games.

- Research was also carried out on Harrogate's home pitch to establish how it normally played. This might indicate what adjustments they would have to make.

- There were two postponements but Harrogate travelled on the first occasion. Casual conversation on this occasion indicated that their players might be somewhat apprehensive about the slower nature of Wolverhampton's pitch.

Result:

Harrogate 172 for 8   Wolverhampton 173 for 3

This was another inspired performance! Research contributed, however, it was how the players performed on the day that mattered.

Preparation:

The psychology of our preparation was again important. The team talk included the virtues we would need. Added to patience, determination, self-control and self-belief - the word "bottle". The four best teams in the country are not here by chance and any of them are capable of winning the cup. So "bottle" is vital.

Targeting particular batters paid dividends. It helped to focus the mind, while one-to-one conversation made a significant contribution to the mental preparation of individual players.

The Final

Teddington (Lords)

Tasks: **The arrangements for the final**

- Following the semi-final, Mark Campkin the "Competitions Manager" for the ECB sent a four-page document that contained a lot of information. This information included:
- Notification of teams
- Team reporting on arrival
- Hours of play
- Fitness of Conditions of Play
- Over Rate
- Tossing for Innings
- Pre-Match Practice
- Spectators cars
- Organising Committee
- Dressing Room Attendants
- Public Address System
- Rearrangements of Final
- Coaches
- Tickets
- Bars
- Scorecards
- Photographs
- Advertising
- Equipment
- Movement Behind Bowler's Arm
- Use of Pavilion
- Club Colours
- Dressing Rooms
- Scorers
- Lunches and Teas
- Ground Admission
- Accommodation
- Eve of Final Dinner
- Hospitality

My major consideration was the fact that the Wolverhampton team were young and had an average age of under 24 with six of the squad under 19, which made it crucial that they were psychologically well prepared for such a big occasion.

The main thing that we needed to do was to create an "Action Plan", reproduced on the next page.

I needed to:

- Discuss with the captain - "getting the build-up right"
- Spy on the Ealing versus Teddington semi-final at Ealing

  (Sunday 22nd August)
- Contact Penn C. C. to see if we could have a meeting and practice on the Tuesday before the Friday final (31st August) as Penn had a sloping pitch.
- Visit Mark Campkin - Competitions Manager at the ECB
- Prepare notes on the opposition
- Meet with captain to discuss arrangements and tactics
- Arrange a team meeting with the squad at Penn

Some of the tasks were overlapping but what follows are the main points.

- Following its receipt of the above letter, a detailed list of questions was compiled of issues that particularly affected the players. The object was that there would be no question asked by a player for which there wasn't an answer. It didn't matter if it was to do with the hotel, with pre-match details, with family and friends, with Lord's or with the match itself.
- Mark Campkin was then asked if the club chairman and I could come to London to check out a few arrangements. This request was agreed and we met Mark on the Thursday eight days before the match.
- Important matters were clarified as to which pitch had been allocated, the expectations of the hosts for the day, the MCC, and with the timing of events such as tossing up and pre-match photographs.
- It was at this meeting that photocopies of all of Teddington's scorecards were obtained as well as scorecards from the previous twelve finals, and a mobile number obtained to report our arrival and to be available for general troubleshooting purposes.
- It was at this meeting that a vital request was made that we have a net on the Thursday afternoon before the Friday Final.

The ground

- It was important to approach the preparation for this game in our

ACTION PLAN FOR THE
NATIONAL CLUB CHAMPIONSHIP FINAL

- Discuss with captain "Getting the build-up right".
- Spy on the Ealing versus Teddington semi-final at Ealing
  on Sunday 22nd August.
- Contact Penn C. C. to see if we could have a meeting
  and a square practice on the Tuesday (31st August) before the final.
- Visit Mark Campkin – Competitions Manager at the ECB.
- Prepare notes on the opposition.
- Meet with captain to discuss arrangements and tactics.
- Team Meeting with the selected squad at Penn C.C.

Agenda for the team meeting at Penn C. C.
- Flip chart diagram of Hilton Hotel and Lord's – explanation.
- 6-minute video of Lord's – no sound track – improvise.
- Discuss slope and adjustments that have to be made by batters,
  bowlers, fielders, wicket keeper and captain.
- Set up a simulated practice batting in pairs and all bowlers having a
  go from both ends. Fielders to rotate.
- Go through/distribute itinerary and rooming arrangements
  (See players beforehand to check that they are happy with
  rooming suggestions).
- Final travel arrangements for Thursday 2nd September.

Practice session on Thursday 2nd September on the Lord's Nursery Ground
  Main points:
- Kit to be left in dressing room overnight.
- Relaxed net – purpose is to get over the "gar gar" bit and to feel
  comfortable in the surroundings.
- Free time until walking as a party to Lord's for the per-match dinner.
  Main danger – "free drinks"!! Quiet word in appropriate ears –
  get senior players to keep a look out.

The final- September 3rd
- Breakfast as a team.
- Walk to the ground as a team.
- Warm-up on Nursery Ground – as close to normal warm-up as
  possible. Ask permission on Thursday to use edge of Nursery
  Ground square.
- Team chat on the Lord's outfield in full view of pavilion before going
  back to the dressing rooms, photographs and tossing of the coin.
- Team chat to be finalised on Thursday.

usual manner. The process needed to be the same.

- The context, however, was different. This was Lord's and for this group of players it was the opportunity of a lifetime.

- Four of the fourteen-man squad had played at Lord's but this still left ten younger players who had not. The challenge was how to prepare them so that they would be able to perform to optimum levels on the day of the final. This required one extra event - a pre-match briefing and practice.

- After the meeting with Mark Campkin, a six-minute video, without commentary, was made to show the players who had not been to Lord's what it looked like. This included the changing rooms, route to wicket via the long room, close up of the likely pitch, shots which indicated the slope of the ground, views around the ground, the media centre, where the box was for family and friends and where the spectators would be. Also included were the Lord's shop, the ECB headquarters, the indoor cricket school, the nursery ground and net practice facilities. This 6-minute video was for the players pre-match briefing and practice at Penn

- Armed with all the information, a full itinerary was constructed. See end of chapter. The purpose of the itinerary was that there was something tangible for the players, especially the younger players, to hang onto when events were going on all around them.

The pre-match briefing and practice

- Based on the video, I constructed a hand drawn sketch of Lord's and the situation of the hotel onto a flip chart. See next page. I contacted Penn Cricket Club, a local team in Wolverhampton with whom we had a number of connections, to see if we could hold a meeting and a square practice on the Tuesday before the final. Penn had a slope, which was greater than Lord's but it did give a flavour of the adjustments that would be required.

Agenda for team meeting:

- Flip chart diagram of Hilton Hotel and Lords. To show and explain the details contained on the flip chart of where everything was situated at Lords and to relate this to the geographical position of the hotel.

- To show the 6 minute video and to make an improvised commentary to explain what was on screen.

- To discuss the slope and the adjustments that bowlers, batters and fielders would have to make. This then led into the practice. The

meeting continued after the practice to tidy up
administrative arrangements.

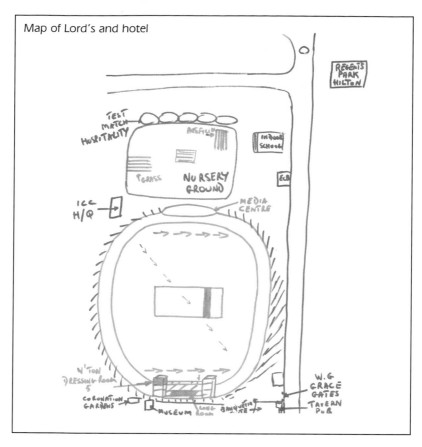

Map of Lord's and hotel

The practice

- A kwik cricket blue extra stump was placed on the upper side of the
  wickets as this seemed to be the best way of indicating how much
  adjustment was required. The danger was to avoid over stating the
  difficulty. The bowlers were asked to regard the blue wicket as real,
  so when bowling from the pavilion end, the middle stump was the
  real leg stump and the leg stump didn't exist, and when bowling from
  the media centre end, the middle stump was off stump and the off
  stump didn't exist. (This assumed right handed batters.)

- All the bowlers had a try from each end to see who felt comfortable
  or uncomfortable at the point of delivery. The batters worked in
  pairs to experience the slight shift in weight distribution and the
  likely areas that the ball would go off the bat.

- The fielders experienced the different angles that they had to take into account and to get a feel as to which way the ball was likely to drift off the bat.

- The captain was able to get a feel for the adjustment to field placings that would be required for orthodox batting, and this led to a strategy of who we thought would bowl and from which end. At this stage it was a "what if" strategy based on the indications that we would be playing on a pitch quite close to the Tavern stand. In the event this was not required because we were subsequently allocated pitch 13 for the final and this produced a 60-yard boundary to the Tavern stand. (And guess what my lucky number is? yes 13)

Team meeting (continued) after the above practice.

- The full itinerary was distributed to the players and explained, where necessary, along with the rooming arrangements that had been discussed prior to publication. The room pairings proved positive, supportive ("buddy") and successful.

- The final travel arrangements were discussed

The opposition

- Rain had caused the postponement of not only our semi-final but also that of Teddington and Ealing. We were able to play our match and leave almost three weeks for preparation while Teddington were left with less than two weeks because their semi-final was played a week later. This was to our advantage because there was less of a rush and it also made it possible to watch the Ealing versus Teddington semi-final at Ealing and to make notes on each of their players. This proved very useful. The long journey was worth it for many reasons, but none less than having a strategy in place as to how to bowl to a particular batsman who was unorthodox and potentially a match winner.

- The visit of the club chairman and myself to Lord's to see Mark Campkin was after the Teddington semi-final and the full scorecards obtained enabled our normal analysis of the opposition to take place. The emphasis in the analysis was on who played in the latter rounds, how players were used and who had been the form players throughout the competition.

The day prior to the match

- There was a reasonably relaxed journey to Lord's although traffic near to London delayed us a little. We were able to drop off our main luggage at the Regent's Park Hilton ready for checking in later and travel on the coach, complete with cricket kit, the 400 yards to the W. G. Grace gate. A further short 100-yard walk to the pavilion entrance, up two flights of stairs and there we were in dressing room 5 overlooking the ground.

- The whole afternoon was deliberately low key. The object was to try and get as much as possible of the "gar-gar" and spellbound emotions out of the system. We needed time for the players to "drink in" the view of Lord's from the balcony and to locate all the areas of the ground that they had seen on the video. We changed slowly giving time to look at the performance boards for centuries and 5 wickets in a match. The nervous excitement was pretty high.

- Walking well to the side of the square, as had been requested; we walked across Lord's, underneath the media centre and to the grass nets.

- The weather was magnificent and exactly the same was predicted for the final. This meant that the messages about dehydration and proper eating at the evening pre-match dinner, at breakfast and in our pre-match preparations could be emphasised. I needn't have concerned myself, as that was one agenda item that had become part of our routine. This also applied to our routines connected with skin protection.

- The practice went well with everyone in good spirits. Some had a grass net while others had throw downs. Bowlers bowled well within themselves. The opportunity to have a number of one-to-one discussions was taken.

- As we returned to the dressing room, I paced out the short boundary and discovered that it was about 60 yards. This meant that we could bowl the bowlers from the more logical ends and the spinner had some room to play with.

- Players changed and hung up their kit ready for the final and then did their own thing. (To be able to leave kit overnight in the dressing room was a big bonus and one less thing to be concerned about on the day of the match.) The time between 4.00p.m. and 7.00p.m. was free. Some went back to the hotel while others explored the stands and media centre by doing a circuit of the ground. The view from the media centre, by the way, is awesome.

- At 7.00p.m. the players, relatives and friends met in the hotel reception and walked the short distance to the Banqueting Suite at Lord's. The knowledge that the drinks would be complimentary set off one or two alarm bells in my head, but having a few quiet words with the senior players had eased these. They kept an eye out on the younger players and helped to ensure that the evening was enjoyable and yet not damaging to our preparation.

The day of the match

• The itinerary at the end of the chapter details the complete schedule but the important thing was that we had breakfast as a team, we met in reception as a team and we walked to the ground as a team.

• I didn't want the players to have to worry about the schedule of events and the players for their part were quite happy just to do as requested.

• On the previous day I had approached the ground staff to ask if we could finish off our warm up with bowlers using the edge of the nursery ground square as we wanted to warm up in as close a way to normal as possible. They were delighted to be consulted rather than taken for granted and they couldn't have been more helpful. The ground staff even remarked that this was the same as Gloucestershire had done in their two successful finals.

• We made no changes to our typical warm up and finished with a team chat (see next page) sitting in the shade in full view of the inspirational main pavilion.

• Following the toss, which we lost, and the official photographs, the players withdrew to the dressing room to get ready to field. Fielding was an advantage in the sense that we were all together supporting each other in the first few tense overs. This was later to be of advantage when batting. What was required was quite clear.

• Most of my job had been done. It only remained to make sure that the one-to-one discussions were appropriate and directed towards the players who needed them during the second half of the game. For one it would be just eye contact and a nod of understanding, to another "well bowled" knowing that would be enough to set them up for their all-rounder role, to another "Ok? Need anything?", while to another a more spelt out description of what was required. Some needed to be left alone while some needed to be involved in conversation. See chapter 4 on Communication.

• The other role was to support players who were out, reassuring them of their contribution. For some it would be "You did an excellent job, now help the players who still have to bat". For another who was very disappointed, it would be to reflect on performances that were crucial in us getting to the final and for this to be the springboard for them also supporting the players who were still to bat. This also applied to a player who was the victim of a run-out mix-up at the wicket.

• After joining in the initial dressing room celebrations we went down to the presentation area. It was at this point that I chose to leave the players to celebrate on their own. They went to the gardens behind

TEAM CHAT FOR
THE NATIONAL CLUB CHAMPIONSHIP FINAL

• Usual format – captain and coach working together

• Main points for team talk

• Usual pointers of the opposition

• Concentrate on what we do

• Remind about the priorities we agreed pre-season

       Team/Units

       Preparation

       Mental Toughness

       Mental Focus (Including being ready for opposition "chat")

       Enjoyment

• Remind re qualities we require that have served us well

       Patience

       Determination

       Self-control

       Self-belief

       "Bottle"

• Keep it simple – 270 balls – one by one

• Bowlers – keep it in the right places

the pavilion to be photographed while I decided to thank as many as possible of the hundreds of supporters. It was a very pleasant and appropriate way to wind down a little. In any case I wanted the players to take centre stage. See the end of chapter 6 for a more detailed explanation of my views about the role of the coach. After the evening celebrations, the journey back and the end of season party, it felt like weeks before the floating on air feeling subsided.

Result	**Teddington 185 for 7 (45 overs)**
	Wolverhampton 189 for 6 (44 overs)

This was yet another inspired performance despite the pressure of the situation.

Preparation: There is absolutely no doubt in my mind that the preparation described had a major effect on the performance. By the time we reached the final, the squad took for granted the way that we approached things. The detail was accepted as being part and parcel of how and why quality performance was produced during match play.

The satisfaction of being coach to the winners of the National Club Championship cannot be measured and the scorecard reprinted on the next page will remain a trigger for a thousand happy memories.

The trials and tribulations that followed during the following season only served to show how success in cricket, like all other sports, and for that matter life itself, is not a permanent state! Cricket is not immune from the ups and downs that accompany survival on this planet, and it helps for a coach to philosophically accept this fact. Every year brings new challenges, a new squad to mould together, new team confidence to develop, past success to emulate - and despite equal commitment from the coach, it can go wrong. It did in the year 2000.

3 – So how did we try to make things happen in league matches during 2000 when the team were relatively unsuccessful?

This is a painful process to recount. What follows is drawn from the notes made in preparation for each league match, and, in some cases, recollections of how I felt after the match.

The overall method of preparation was the same as for the successful seasons in 1998 and 1999. The difference was not in the preparation that I made prior to the match, but in what was communicated to the players and how it was delivered.

It is important to recognise that the playing conditions were totally different from the win, winning draw, losing draw, and bonus point system of 1998 and 1999. The playing conditions (chosen from a menu of ECB

MARYLEBONE CRICKET CLUB

 LORD'S GROUND

NATIONAL CLUB CHAMPIONSHIP – FINAL
TEDDINGTON v. WOLVERHAMPTON

FRIDAY, 3rd SEPTEMBER, 1999   (1-day Match – 45 overs)

TEDDINGTON   Innings

1	M. A. Crawley	not out	101
2	T. W. Harrison	st Mackelworth b Connelly	13
3	R. O. Jones	c Ahmed b Heap	45
7	N. D. Martin	c Bradford b Griffiths	1
†4	J. M. Attfield	b Griffiths	3
6	A. P. Tarrant	b Griffiths	4
8	J. C. Barrett	run out	0
10	C. M. Pitcher	b Ahmed	0
9	S. D. Weale	not out	3
5	R. J. Ballinger		
*11	A. C. Harlow		
		B , l-b 5, w 10, n-b	15

Total ....(7 wkts, 45 overs) 185

FALL OF THE WICKETS
1—35 2—136 3—142 4—160 5—176 6—178 7—178 8— 9— 10—

ANALYSIS OF BOWLING

Name	O.	M.	R.	W.	Wd.	N-b.
Heap	9	3	23	1	1	...
Connelly	9	0	27	1	5	...
Grifftihs	9	0	33	3	...	...
Anders	9	0	36	0	...	...
Ahmed	9	0	61	1	1	...
	...	...	...	...	...	...

WOLVERHAMPTON   Innings

1	C. Tranter	lbw b Crawley	48
2	J. V. Anders	c Martin b Barrett	46
3	G. D. Wright	c Harlow b Crawley	8
†4	D. J. Lampitt	c Ballinger b Weale	34
5	T. M. Heap	b Harrison	16
6	R. J. Bradford	run out	9
*7	A. N. Mackelworth	not out	6
8	S. N. Lycett	not out	0
9	T. J. Connelly		
10	S. Ahmed		
11	P. Griffiths		
		B , l-b 4, w 17, n-b 1,	22

Total ....(6 wkts, 44 overs) 189

FALL OF THE WICKETS
1—98 2—116 3—123 4—153 5—172 6—185 7— 8— 9— 10—

ANALYSIS OF BOWLING

Name	O.	M.	R.	W.	Wd.	N-b.
Ballinger	3	0	18	0	4	1
Harrison	9	1	30	1	4	...
Pitcher	6	0	21	0	1	...
Weale	9	0	45	1	3	...
Barrett	9	0	37	1	1	...
Crawley	8	0	34	2	3	...

Umpires—Steve Bishopp & Martin Armitage   Scorers—M. Keightly & M. L. Chapman
†Captain   *Wicket-keeper
Play begins at 11.00   Luncheon Interval between innings   Close of play 6 p.m.
Teddington won the toss

Wolverhampton won by 4 wickets

Runs per over													
TEDDINGTON	1	2	3	4	5	6	7	8	9	10	11	12	13
14	15	16	17	18	19	20	21	22	23	24	25	26	27	28	29
30	31	32	33	34	35	36	37	38	39	40	41	42	43	44	45
WOLVERHAMPTON	1	2	3	4	5	6	7	8	9	10	11	12	13
14	15	16	17	18	19	20	21	22	23	24	25	26	27	28	29
30	31	32	33	34	35	36	37	38	39	40	41	42	43	44	45

proposals) were crucial to the season and in essence were:

18 points for a win

5 points for a tie

0 points for a defeat (plus bonus points)

2 points for a draw   (plus bonus points)

2 points for an abandoned game with no play

2 points for an abandoned game with play (plus bonus points)

2 points to the side batting 1st and declaring, at or prior to the
  end of the 55th over, provided they have scored a minimum
  total of 150

Bonus points:

Bowling: 1 point up to a maximum of 4 points awarded at 3, 5, 7 and
         9 wickets

Batting: 1 point up to a maximum of 4 points awarded at 100, 150, 200
         and 250 runs.

The match was 110 overs with the side batting first able to bat for 60 overs. If, however, they bowled their overs quickly, then on the basis of time, they could bowl more than the minimum 50 back. (Not easy to manage from a tactical point of view especially if you have more than one strong spinner.)

There were anomalies, the most important of which was that in a reduced over game, the declaration requirements were the same as for a full game.

I thought that I had looked thoroughly at the implications of the new playing regulations, but it is not only the coach who must understand them. This has implications for communication with the team and will be discussed in more detail in chapter 4 "Communication". It became obvious, more than once, that the awareness level of some players as to how to maximise points under the new system was incomplete.

Chapter 2, "Preparation" referred to the bold strategy of Wolverhampton Cricket Club "going it alone" without an overseas player. In my own mind, I was certain that we had the capability of finishing mid-table. The overseas player, in my opinion, was the addition that would be required if the club were to strive for top honours. Given time, it would be possible, I believed, for the club to be both self-sufficient and strive for top honours.

The club went for self-sufficiency following a request from the previous overseas player to be released from his contract for the 2000 season. He was released and the pre-season meeting schedule referred to in chapter 2 was followed. The meeting with the captain and then the captain and vice-captain contained some doubt about the ability of the batters to adapt to the new situation and to manage without the overseas batter and this pre-season doubt, on reflection, was to be an important component of the teams self belief.

This issue was addressed in the pre-season meeting of players. Although this is strictly "Preparation" it is recounted here because of its importance to the malfunctioning season.

I had analysed the 1999 season in performance terms and especially drew attention to batting and bowling. The fact that 26.2% of our runs had been scored by the overseas player, James Henderson, plus two innings (registered players) from Paul Pollard and one innings from Vikram Solanki. I stressed my belief that the team were up to the task of replacing the 26.2% and that our accepted bowling strength would support the batters by making it hard for the opposition to score runs, especially when it was backed up by our customary top quality fielding. The meeting included much more but the above gives the context.

What follows is a match-by-match account of team talks and outcome. The detailed preparation for each match followed the pattern previously described in successful seasons and the all-important one-to-one discussions continued as before. After the 22nd and final match, there is a section on "Post season reflections".

Match 1	Away match against Old Hill. Abandoned (Only two matches played, one of which turned out to be our opponents in match 2.
Match 2	Home match lost to West Bromwich Dartmouth (Toss lost)
Team talk	I stressed that in the previous season, three players had scored most of their runs and two had left the club, and that three people got their wickets and only two remained.
Outcome	This was a poor batting performance lacking grit and determination, but it was our first time on grass due to the extremely wet pre-season. Perhaps it was the first sign of batting frailty. Opposition strength relied heavily on the batting of Warwickshire's Wagh (62) in chasing a low total. (112)
Match 3	Away match lost to Walsall (Toss lost)
Team talk	Sign of a good side is that they bounce back. This is the winning National Knockout team other than for

one player.

We have a good track record against Walsall. They are only 4 points above us. (And then pointed out the opposition targets players.)

Reminder about the qualities required:

PATIENCE

DETERMINATION

SELF-CONTROL

SELF-BELIEF

Control the controllable, stay positive and enjoy the challenge.

Outcome	A below par batting performance overall with a declaration coming early to gain bonus points. The captain and I agreed that we needed to secure as many bonus points as possible. They would be important to final league position. Little did we know at the time how important!
Match 4	Home match against Coventry and North Warwick. (Toss lost)
	(abandoned half way)
Team talk	Highlighted key opposition targets and then emphasised:
	Concentrate on every ball
	Application and commitment
	Focus on your job
Outcome	An encouraging and much improved batting display
Match 5	Home match against Halesowen. Abandoned. No-one played.
Match 6	Away match drawn against Harborne. (Toss lost)
Team talk	Highlighted key opposition targets and emphasised the same points as for match 4 adding a tactical awareness of the angles and shape of a small ground by holding the team meeting on the shortest boundary.
Outcome	A batting performance rescued by an experienced no. 8

leading to a strong finishing position. Fielding angles well defended but a lot of catches put down, normally our strongest card. There was a need to emphasise fielding and concentration on the next practice night.

Match 7	Away match against Cannock. Abandoned. Only one match played.
Match 8	Home match drawn against Kidderminster. (Toss won)
Team talk	This was in response to the downbeat talk of some players.

1. Control the controllable

i. You can't control the weather, and when the sun comes out or cloud cover appears

ii. You can't control the toss

iii. You can't control the order of the fixture list

iv. You can't control who we play and who we are abandoned against

v. You can't control injury except in a limited way

vi. You can't control overseas availability. (Kidderminster professional arrived the day before the match)

vii. You can't control illness

viii. You can't control availability except to a limited extent

ix. You can't control the decisions of umpires

x. You can't control who is bowling when you go into bat or the batter you bowl at when the captain asks you to bowl.

xi. You can't control the strength of the opposition on a particular day, especially the availability or non-availability of contracted and allocated registered players

xii. You can't control what shifts have to be worked e.g. our captain and vice-captain having to do night duty.

2. WE control what WE do. WE get out what WE put in.

3. It is true that a number of things have gone against us. What we need at the moment is "street fighters. Bat with conviction, bowl with conviction, field EVERY ball – don't get caught napping.

4. Think TEAM

5. We are top 6 material

6. Take personal responsibility

7. QUALITY CRICKET PRODUCES QUALITY RESULTS

The above was delivered in a theatrical and inspirational way to try and ignite a spark. There is more on "Controlling the Controllable" in chapter 4 'Team Communication'.

Outcome A very good response initially but it slipped towards the end of the innings and they got away due to fielding lapses. Batting should have secured maximum points but was just below the mark and we finished 7 short! I was a bit concerned that the team talk hadn't done the trick. This match should have been won. It was a watershed day, which could have avoided a lot on anguish later on in the season.

Match 9 Away match won against Smethwick.
(Toss won)

Team talk This is a crunch game, the first in a sequence of 6. Smethwick are on their knees at the moment and we must keep them there. We need to show our National Knockout spirit.

Outcome We did what we needed to do and secured a much needed boost to confidence.

Match 10 Home match lost against Stratford.
(Toss lost)

Team talk Stratford are a good batting side. We must bowl accurately backed up by quality fielding. We must also put in a top batting performance. There was a move away from focussing on opposition target players and more towards "getting our own act together". What WE do is all-important.

Outcome A stuttering batting performance lacking in confidence generally. Bowled out without using all available overs. Easy chase for Stratford.

Match 11 Home match drawn against Barnt Green
(Reduced overs) (Toss lost)

Team talk	Mentioned opposition players but concentrated on the theme of PARTNERSHIPS – in batting in pairs with application, and in bowling together with concentration and solid back up in the field.
Outcome	A good performance in the conditions with both bat and ball. Reaction of captain to umpiring decision regarding weather and stoppage of play indicated that he was becoming a bit stressed by events.
Match 12	Away match lost against Stratford. (Toss lost)
Team talk	This is the second half of the season starting today. It's a chance for a new beginning. I challenge you to finish in the top 4 or 5 in this half of the season, which means winning about 4 games. I will keep a separate league table for this half of the season. (The players accepted this challenge.) Reminder that quality cricket = quality results.
Outcome	A very disappointing batting display in a reduced over game. There was an apparent lack of awareness about the need to reach a batting target in order to secure bonus points for batting and declaring. We were two runs and one ball short of 3 extra bonus points! Weather conditions favoured the Stratford run chase.
Match 13	Home match drawn against Old Hill (Toss won)
Team talk	Decided to keep it very simple. We need a good performance today. Each of you needs to concentrate on your job.
Outcome	Although the match was drawn, there was some fighting qualities displayed.
Match 14	Away match lost against Barnt Green (Toss lost)
Team talk	THIS IS IT. Barnt Green are the team immediately above us. We need total commitment. No second chance with this game. We need batting partnerships. We cannot control the fact that Driver is playing due

to Worcestershire's match lasting only 3 days!

Outcome A magnificent innings from the captain but the innings fell away because the support players "switched off" when things were going well and performed badly when they were needed. The presence of Driver was crucial to the result. His bowling and batting contribution made all the difference. This was a bad blow to the confidence of the team, which led to three more defeats in the next four games! This was a tough time for the coach and the captain.

Note: **At this stage of the season, the captain decided to stand down. He believed that there was a need for an injection of new blood and enthusiasm. His vice-captain took over and he asked another player to act as his vice-captain.**

Match 15 Away match lost against West Bromwich Dartmouth. (Toss lost)

Team talk For the first time, I asked for the team talk to take place before the warm up. This was in order to ask for total support for the new captain if we were to pull ourselves out of our poor league position. **After asking for total support for the captain.** THIS IS IT - AGAIN. The Dartmouth are the next team in our sights. Again, we can only control what we do and how we perform. It is out of our control that Wagh and Sheikh are free from Warwickshire commitments and are able to play. It is getting tough and we must recognise that opposition teams are going to pull out all the stops at this time of the season. Wagh and Sheikh have to be our main targets. The rest of the team have limitations. Let's concentrate on what WE do, and do it well.

Outcome A game dominated by Wagh and Sheikh. They took 90% of the wickets and scored 76% of the runs!

Match 16 Home game drawn against Walsall. (Toss lost)

Team talk We know all about our local rivals. Let's give them a real run for their money. The captain asked the team to be no more the "Mr. Nice Guys" of the league.

Outcome	A determined performance with many players doing their bit. The batting was solid for 60 overs and the bowling and fielding powerful and well directed until Walsall decided to play for the draw. This brought out the worst in the team. Although I recognised we were fighting for our premiership survival, I didn't believe that this was the right way to do it, and I left the players in no doubt about my feelings. It was not the Wolverhampton way.
Match 17	Away game lost against Coventry and North Warwick. (Toss lost)
Team talk	We have 6 games left and need to target three wins. Why not today for the first? What we need is the Walsall hardness without losing our cool. Go out there and enjoy it and play the quality cricket you know you are capable of playing.
Outcome	Coventry chose to bat. We played quality, tight cricket for 50 overs and then let it slip in the last 10 on a hot day, and then the batting fell away and lacked overall determination. (See the note below, which affected the players.) There was still a great last wicket rearguard, which succeeded for 12 overs and finished just 6 balls short of a much-needed draw and 2 more points.

Note: It was after the Coventry and North Warwick innings that another devastating blow hit Wolverhampton. The players believed that everything had gone against us during the season and that nothing more could possibly go wrong. They were wrong. Our scorer, Mary Chapman, lost her balance as she was leaving the scorebox and fell about five feet from the descending steps. Severe injuries required an ambulance to take Mary to hospital where she subsequently had to receive almost two hours of surgery for injuries to her left arm.

Note: It was at this stage of the season that I could feel the chances of turning the team round diminishing by the game. It was time to try something more dramatic: something to provide new drive, new incentive, new belief, and new desire. What follows below was in effect almost my "last throw of the dice". I felt as if I had given everything I had and yet had still failed to get the players to perform. Provided we could get out of jail, we could learn from the experience and be stronger in the future.

TO OUR FIRST TEAM SQUAD

I have taken the step of writing to you because I feel that while you are hearing what I say, some appear to have stopped listening. I generalise I know and take that risk.

You may not agree with all that I say but I ask you to read this open letter.

We are not dead.

22-match season, 4 abandoned, 18 played if no more abandoned

5 matches left 5/18 is a highly significant 28% of all matches

There are 90 points still available at 18 per win

It is true that we have had a lot of things go against us, but they have been mostly out of our control. We have also lost games that we should have drawn, drawn games that we should have won, and missed out on bonus points that we should have achieved. That, however, is history.

Collectively we must do everything within our control to fight for our survival. We must fight for every point we can scrape together.

Some of you believe we are doomed and it shows – if this is the case you should not make yourself available for selection.

Some of you are thinking about where you will play next year, even worse talking to other players about it – if this is the case you should not make yourself available for selection.

There is no room for anyone who isn't fully committed to the fight for survival.

What remains?

Saturday 19th Aug	12.30 start	Halesowen	Away
Saturday 26th Aug	12.30 start	Harborne	Home
Monday 28th Aug	12.30 start	Cannock	Home

Saturday 2nd Sept   12.00 start   Kidderminster   Away
Saturday 9th Sept   12.00 start   Smethwick   Home

You will note that through a quirk of the fixture list 3 of the last 4 games are against other basement teams.

Tim Heap has asked Greg Wright to act as vice-captain for the remainder of the season so let's give the new leadership the support it deserves.

We have said in the past that in times of crisis it is our team bonding that will see us through. We have lost sight of this a bit with players ready to criticise others.

It is the responsibility of each and every player to support every player.

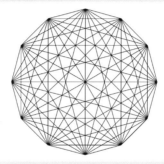

We also need to commit afresh to our agreed priorities:

TEAM SPIRIT – WORKING IN UNITS

PREPARATION

MENTAL STRENGTH (toughness)

MENTAL FOCUS (concentration)

ENJOYMENT

And to our track record of recognising the importance of:

PATIENCE

DETERMINATION

SELF-CONTROL

SELF-BELIEF

and, at this moment, BOTTLE.

Let's not hang our hat of this excuse or that excuse. Lets take responsibility for our own performance and never give up no matter what events unfold. Let's do it.

Match 18	Away match narrowly lost against Halesowen. (Toss lost)
Team talk	The open letter said it all. We must have a batting base. Go out and do it.
Outcome	A very spirited performance. However, after a solid base, the batting fell away again leaving a modest total to defend. We almost did it. There were at last some glimmers of team determination and team spirit and team belief in the performance. There were the seeds of optimism about the four matches left, especially as three were against lower half of the league teams.
Match 19	Home match abandoned against Harborne (Toss won)
Team talk	We all know that this is a "must win" situation. Let's go out and do it. We know where they are coming from and it's obvious what they want. They would prefer the match to be abandoned but if not, then they will try and stop us from winning. If they bat first they will want to declare to gain extra points. They will be anxious whereas we have little to lose. Note: This match was delayed due to rain, and in a 'kick about' the captain fractured his arm. The Vice captain took over and the coach became 12th man!
Outcome	This was a hard working performance with a depleted bowling attack. The score to chase was kept within reasonable limits. The chase was on course when rain caused the game to be abandoned. The mood in the Harborne camp was high and in Wolverhampton's low. We had played much better for the second successive match and still had nothing to show for it.
Match 20	Home match drawn against Cannock (Toss won)
Team talk	We are back to a "must win" situation. It's us that matter today not Cannock. They are trying to win a championship and will also want to win. We might well get a chance because of their need for points.

Outcome	We were disappointed with our seam bowling performance and were left with more than we should to chase. At one stage we were on course for victory, but it slipped away at the death. Most of the team probably believed that the chances of survival were slim. What was certainly true was that it was no longer only in our own hands.

Match 21	Away match won against Kidderminster (Toss lost)
Team talk	We must win, it's as simple as that. We are 28 points adrift of West Bromwich Dartmouth and 29 adrift of Harborne and there are a maximum 40 points available and that means batting first and declaring. We need to be really positive. Kidderminster have no contracted players.
Outcome	This was probably the best performance of the year. We were put into bat, scored our runs quickly, declared and then bowled Kidderminster out. Maximum 20 points achieved - half way there as far as what we could do. It all seemed so simple. Just how we used to do it. In addition, West Bromwich Dartmouth and Harborne, as well as Wolverhampton, were well aware that our last match was against Smethwick who were already relegated. Anxiety would be eating away at our target teams.

Match 22	Home match won against Smethwick (Toss lost)
Team talk	I've got all the detail concerning the West Bromwich Dartmouth and Harborne games, but it means nothing until we have done our business. This is as big a game for the club as the National Knockout final last year or two years ago when we needed to beat Kidderminster to win the league. Assuming we bat, we need a solid base of say 170/180+ in about 45 overs if possible to leave us with 65 back to both bowl Smethwick out and give ourselves cover should it rain.
Outcome	It went better than expected scoring 240 before the

first wicket fell at which point we declared after 34 overs leaving us a massive 76 overs in which to bowl Smethwick out. Because our declaration had come so early, we had to have an hours play before tea. During this hour, we played with anxiety and the situation proved difficult as we went for the jugular and probably over attacked. After tea, however, we went back to more normal play and wrapped up the innings in 29.4 overs.

It then became a telephone strewn, tense two hours as first the news that West Bromwich Dartmouth had secured the eight points they needed, to be followed some time later by the news that Barnt Green were in a strong position to beat Harborne. After what seemed like an eternity, the news came through that Harborne had lost to Barnt Green and finished one point behind us in the league table.

There were celebrations, but they were celebrations of relief. Time was needed to reflect on the season and to plan for 2001.

POST-SEASON REFLECTIONS

As I write this between the 2000 and 2001 seasons, it helps to persuade the inner self that hard times in life make you stronger! The experience of avoiding relegation in 2000 wasn't fun, but survival can be satisfying for a coach if only in a masochistic sort of way!

What I was reminded of during the season was the presentation that Frank Dick made at "Cricket Live - 1999" (7) when he referred to "Mountain People" and "Valley People". When the going became tough it was the "Mountain People" that the coach needed in the team. Players who were prepared to live on the edge, to be optimistic and bold and to fight rather than the "Valley People" who talked pessimistically and despondently and looked for excuses and the easy "if only" and succumbed.

The coach will not survive unless he/she is a "Mountain Person" who is prepared to take calculated risks. And yet the coach can only control a certain numbers of parameters. It helps if the coach is philosophical and able to identify what is and isn't controllable. While it is the coach's task to draw the attention of the team to what is controllable and uncontrollable in match situations, it is easy to forget to do the same with him/herself.

Exorcising the ghost

At the end of the season, it was important to let the dust settle. To have an in-depth investigation in September would have been, in my opinion, counterproductive.

It was mentioned earlier that the 1st XI captain had resigned after match 14, and that new leadership had plotted the route to survival. It was natural to assume therefore that the same captain and vice captain that finished the 2000 season would be leading in 2001. A meeting between the three of us took place just over two weeks after the end of the league season during which we explored the main issues. These were agreed to be:

- **Club politics**

- **The selection committee process**

- **Playing matters**

Club politics: it would be inappropriate to discuss the internal politics of a club. It was agreed, however, that a number of issues in this area needed attention.

The selection committee process: without going into detail, it was agreed that our selection process could be significantly improved.

Playing matters: the following were discussed ~

- Annual players meeting

- Overseas player

- More flexible use of a squad system

- Liaison between captain, vice-captain and coach re selection matters

- Improvement in player awareness and communication

- Change of practice night

- Players for 2001

- Knock out competitions for 2001

- Relationship between practice and knock outs

- Evaluation of each player in the squad

There were agreed outcomes from the meeting and tasks for each of us to complete.

What we discussed is less important than the fact that we met soon after the season to plan a long-term strategy.

An essential part of that strategy was to hold a meeting to see what lessons needed to be learned. The next captain and vice-captain were keen to do this and that was an important commitment on their part.

The meeting was held on November 15th and scheduled for 6.30p.m. The time was chosen because the England versus France football match was on television later the same evening. It was thought that by combining the two events, it would be possible to discuss the past season and also make it into a social event.

I was asked to take the lead and I decided to follow the same pattern as had successfully been used prior to the 1999 season. See chapter 2 - "Preparation" in the section described in an "Example of a Pre-season Players meeting".

We used the same "open plan" seating arrangement. The players paired up to brainstorm the factors that they thought contributed to the poor performances in 2000. The 25 reasons were listed on a flip chart and then the pairs, following broader discussion of the points on the flip chart, were asked to pick what they thought were the five most important reasons. By scoring a point for each choice we finished with a list of major reasons. There was far less consensus than when determining priorities for future success, but the following five factors came to the top of the list. Of the 25 on the long list, 13 received at least one vote. The full list of reasons is considered a little later. The 5 main reasons were:

1. POOR ATTITUDE AND LACK OF PROFESSIONALISM

2. LOWER TEAM SPIRIT

3. LACK OF CONFIDENCE

4. HIGHER LEVELS OF INJURY

5. NO PROFESSIONAL

It is interesting to compare the above list with the priorities for success from 1999:

WHEN SUCCESSFUL	WHEN UNSUCCESSFUL
Team spirit / Working in units	Lower team spirit
Preparation / Training & practice	Poor attitude to preparation / Lack of professionalism
Mental Strength / (Toughness)	Mental / (Lack of confidence)
Mental Focus (Concentration)	
Enjoyment	
	Higher levels of injury
	No professional

The players themselves recognised that 3 of the factors were fairly closely linked and that lack of enjoyment was the bi-product. And of the other two factors, it was true that there were indeed higher levels of injury especially amongst the seam attack.

The listing of consensus reasons concluded the meeting because everyone was agreed that it had been important to exorcise the ghost so that when we met pre-2001 season we could focus immediately on looking forward and not back. The meeting was a springboard for bouncing positively forward.

Further post players' meeting reflections

The only factor that I didn't agree with was the "No professional". I had said before the 2000 season commenced that the absence of an overseas player would be the difference between being able to aim for league honours and finishing mid-table. In my opinion however, it should not have led to a scrap for survival. We should have finished mid-table irrespective of all the difficulties.

There were lessons for the coach to learn out of the experience. While logically we should have finished mid-table, that opinion was worth nothing if the captain and players didn't believe it. I have had to recognise that the factor of "lack of self-belief" affected the team more than I had appreciated. A reliance on an overseas players isn't what I want for Wolverhampton Cricket Club or English cricket, but it proves to me that the dependency culture I referred to in chapter 2 will take a long while to eradicate.

The absence of an overseas player gave the team, or those who wanted one, an excuse for their own below par performance. Much easier to say that it is the absence of a professional that is the cause of problems than to look in the mirror and accept individual responsibility. Given a choice, a lot of players will 'park' the responsibility outside themselves if they can. Getting players to accept their contribution/responsibility is one of the central tasks of a coach.

Add to this a feeling that some thought that if the team couldn't strive for top honours then "what was the point", and the link to lower commitment and poor performance was easier to see. This type of negative thinking can spread quickly through a team.

In order that I made the most of the player's observations, I decided to analyse the full list of reasons that were suggested at the meeting. Even though an overseas professional has been appointed for 2001, there would still be team and player insights to better understand. It was in January 2001 that I performed this task as part of my preparation for the season ahead.

The list that follows was not the order in which the observations were made. The observations have been listed into what appear to be logical groups. The first stab at placing the observations into categories was into the five ingredients of physical, mental, technical, tactical and lifestyle.

There were no "lifestyle" issues. "Physical" issues related to a higher level of injuries, and "technical" issues to only the comment about the type of pitch and didn't become a major reason for the players. (Pitches during 2000 were predominantly wet.) This left "mental" and "tactical" issues which swallowed up the vast majority of the stated reasons. Here is the full list. The reasons in bold received at least one final vote.

- **Higher level of injuries**
- **Type of pitch (soft & wet)**
- Loss of early wickets
- Lack of partnerships
- Lost too many games which should have been drawn or won
- Lack of encouragement in the field
- Lack of support for each other when the "proverbial hit the fan"
- **No overseas/professional player**
- Players more interested in a laugh than in quality cricket
- Captain & coach short of motivation
- **No chance of winning the league**
- **Poor attitude to practice**
- **Unprofessional - late arrival for matches and attitude to warm-ups**
- **Poor attitude - cocky, arrogant and lazy**
- **Not enough responsibility taken**
- Passing the buck
- Over confidence from 1999
- **Pessimistic vibes from senior players in the early part of the season**
- Hard for new comers to feel part of the team
- **Not enough competition for places**
- Lost best two players - overseas player (batter) and strike bowler to injury
- **Lack of confidence**
- **Team spirit lower**

- **Lack of enjoyment**

- Attitude better in National and County Knockouts

When things go wrong, there are no magical answers, and I'd like to share thoughts with the reader as if we were both sitting in armchairs discussing the issue.

Question - "What went wrong?"

Coach - "It's complicated because people and cricket teams/squads are complicated. Each season there is a different mix of personalities, so what works one year might not work in the next.

Managers of professional football teams who manage a relegation struggle presumably become better at fighting for survival if relegation issues arise again. They learn from experience. They, or the clubs they belong to, develop strategies. In the professional game, sometimes the manager/coach is replaced, sometimes money is thrown at the problem and sometimes a new face brings a fresh perspective in addition to existing resources. In any case the players are being paid and can be expected to work hard for the cause. However, in the predominantly amateur game of cricket at top club level, the best solution must be to try and avoid the situation arising in the first place. There are fewer sanctions to use.

The 2000 season was my first experience of basement survival as either player or coach, but there is a determination to be prepared well if things start to go wrong on a future occasion. Hopefully it won't happen again, but if anything 'wobbly' starts in future I want to be able to identify and intercept the decline before is becomes a "bun fight". I know for sure that it's important to act early in the season and to not keep on waiting and hoping! It's no good everyone at the club (and the opposition) saying, "We/you are too good to go down". If that is what is being said, then action should have been taken earlier to prevent such comment.

The choice of language of the captain, vice-captain, players, administrators and supporters can often be an early clue to the self-doubt being experienced. Body language also tells its own story.

I've learned a lot. I am reminded of the captain who thinks of changing the field but waits one ball too long and pays the price, or who thinks of changing the bowling but waits one over too long and pays the price. The coach, like the captain who follows well-informed intuition, must back his/her own judgement.

If we take the team talk for match 3 for example. It included, "Control the controllable" so even at this early stage my antennae were trying to tell me something. It wasn't until match 8 however, that "Control the controllable" became a major thrust of the team talk. With hindsight, I should have backed my gut feeling and insisted that we have a team discussion in the period between match 3 and 8 to agree a team response to our indifferent performances.

If I'd had the presence of mind, I would have recounted the talk by Bob Woolmer at 'Cricket Live - 1999' (8) when he described the cycle of success in professional cricket, and the characteristics of winning and losing teams. I started to consider whether it would be possible to devise an

"early warning devise" and a "first aid strategy" for getting a team back on track when it applied to top amateur cricket. The exercise I have been through will hopefully stimulate the coach who is trying to "turn

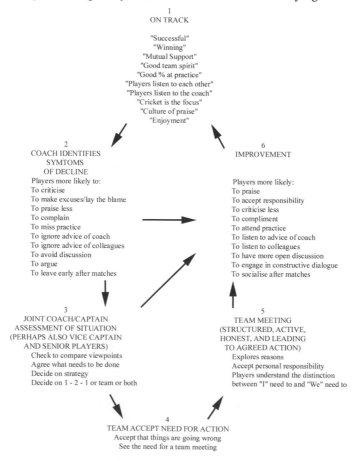

CHAPTER FIVE

things round".

In future I think I will be able to identify the issues more quickly. I share the following thought process. It amounts to a strategy in waiting which I hope I don't have to use in its entirety although parts will probably be used in every season at some time. Every team goes through a patch when it's tough. The best teams however, just like the best players, snap out of their bad patch quicker.

I believe that the essential elements that effect change when things are going wrong can be seen to revolve around six headings:

The diagram on the previous page fills in the detail.

Observation and judgement are not exact sciences, so there is a strong element of intuition and subjectivity, as well as experience, in the following thoughts.

Matters can and are frequently "nipped in the bud" and jump from stage 2 to 6, or with the help of captain and/or vice captain and senior players it can be from 3 to 6. In the worst-case scenario, however, the sequence would be 2-3-4-5-6. *The challenge for the coach is to get the timing right and to make the right judgment as to which route to follow.*

With hindsight, stages 2 moving to 6, or 3 moving to 6, or 3 moving through 4 and 5 to 6 should have occurred earlier. Perhaps then, the last ditch letter prior to match 18 might not have been necessary. I also recognise that as coach I must be more assertive.

The coach cannot "make things happen" on his/her own and needs to recognise the importance of good personal relationships with all players. The captain and senior players, however, are the most important colleagues when it comes to influencing change. Each makes a different contribution, which requires respect even when the coach disagrees with what is being said.

The skills that enable a coach to make the right judgements will depend largely on his/her ability to identify the symptoms of decline (2) and improvement (6).

It is difficult to explain how intuition and instinct contribute to the coach's ability to pick up the "vibes", so it is with some reservation that I suggest that the following are involved:

- A starting point comes from studying the players in the team

- Knowing each player as an individual and how they behave when they are successful

- Knowing how each player behaves when the team is successful

- Noticing changing patterns of behaviour

- Noticing the "tell tale" signs in changing group behaviour
- Changing patterns in interpersonal relationships - who talks with whom?
- Changing patterns in discussion - in front of other team members, or in private
- Observing whether the unsuccessful become distanced
- Listening to conversations between players
- Picking up optimistic and pessimistic use of language
- Picking up expressions of anger, frustration and disapproval
- Picking up the balance of comments (Compare symptoms of decline and improvement)
- Observing the paralanguage including voice (volume), pitch, intensity and speed
- Observing body language including facial expressions, posture and body movements
- Asking open-ended questions in conversations with players
- Recognising changing patterns in the response of players to the coach's advice or team talk.

The above is not a complete list by any means, but hopefully gives a flavour of the sort of "antennae" that the coach needs! The ECB Level II course covers aspects of verbal and non-verbal communication, which contribute valuable insights into this area. The Level III course goes into more detail when it does a lot on developing one-to-one communication techniques and where "attribution" or where players 'park' reasons for success or lack of success.

The reasons for lack of success are particularly significant in the area of the under performing team. Further thoughts in this area can be found in chapter 4 - "Communication" - "The Crucial Factor".

But we did survive! And it should be remembered that it didn't all go wrong. While it is true that league form was very disappointing, we still reached the last eight of the National Club Knock-Out. When overseas players, professionals and registered players from the major counties were excluded from selection, the team immediately had more self-belief, which only went to reinforce the opinion that it was all in the mind.

Question - "How will you prevent it happening again?"

Coach - "I'm not sure that a coach can ever say it won't happen again. There are so many factors within a club that are out of his/her control.

There are many things however, that I will work at to reduce the chances of it happening again.

I can reflect about detail and think that maybe I could have been more specific about what I wanted from each player in a particular game, but the overall principles of my coaching I still believe in. Points like it's no use slamming the whole team for a poor performance when the comments apply to individuals. The causes of underachievement need to be identified and matters resolved collectively or individually as appropriate, although I perhaps need to reflect on the balance I use between stressing the positive (my preference) and giving some players a proverbial 'kick up the backside'.

I mentioned earlier that I first looked at the player's 25 reasons for our poor performance in terms of whether they linked to the physical, mental, technical, tactical or lifestyles dimensions of the game. Having decided that with the exception of physical injuries, and a number of tactical observations, the vast majority of reasons related to mental issues, I looked for further ways to understand what went on.

I returned to resources that had been used in the ECB Level II and Level III courses to explore things further. In the ECB Level II course, the coach is introduced to mental preparation for cricket. It says in an additional resource pack that 'Players must be able to remain focused, maintain emotional control, generate self-confidence and demonstrate commitment', and that's all true. Put another way, players need the 4 'C's - concentration, control, confidence and commitment. See chapter 3 - "Integration" - "The Vital Ingredients" where mental qualities are discussed further.

When the 25 reasons were looked at more closely, then certainly a number came into the category of commitment and confidence, but the issues of control and concentration were also apparent to me as coach. The 4 'C's interrelate in many ways, and yes they enabled me to identify which mental attributes were missing. The next question however, was how to plan to succeed in these areas.

At this stage, I concluded that more shared and agreed goals would probably have made a difference to the level of commitment of the team. My coaching style was addressing the issues of developing individual confidence, concentration and where appropriate, self control, but I hadn't doubted the commitment of individuals and especially the team. The link between mental toughness, commitment and goal setting started to become clearer as I read around the subject. I needed to focus more on the team as an entity as well as on the individuals within the team.

Having revisited ECB Level II resources, I went on to revisit some of the Level III resources and in particular the course text by Bull, Albinson and Shambrook called 'The Mental Game Plan - Getting Psyched for Sport'.

I looked through the list of plans and decided that while I understood and used some of the plans, there were other areas that needed to be developed.

The plans described were:

1. SPORT PSYCHOLOGY - 'The mental toughness plan'

2. DEFINING YOUR GOALS - 'The motivation plan'

3. POSITIVE THINKING - 'The confidence plan'

4. VISUALISATION - 'The imagery plan'

5. ATTENTIONAL CONTROL - 'The concentration plan'

6. ANXIETY CONTROL - 'The arousal management plan'

7. INJURY - 'The recovery plan'

8. GROUP DYNAMICS - 'The team plan'

9. COMPETITION PLAN - 'The professional plan'

10. PUTTING IT ALL TOGETHER - 'The final game plan'

I then went on to read the workbook that was written by Dr. Steve Bull for the ECB level III course to be used in consultation with the Mental Game Plan book. Its sub title was 'A Cricket Coach's 7 step guide'.

Time will tell, but the conclusions I have come to are that in order to minimise a repeat of the 2000 experience at league level, I need to think more about defining our goals (The motivation plan) and more about group dynamics (The team plan). In terms of the 7-step guide, I need to focus more on Step 1 'Mental toughness and commitment' - establishing a strong foundation and Step 2 - 'Goal setting and profiling' - providing purpose and direction. If this can be added to a greater understanding of the six point "early warning device" described earlier, then I am confident that a repeat of season 2000 is unlikely.

Up to this point, I have taken the responsibility for most of the shortcomings of the 2000 season. There are other factors however that should be considered and questions that I have to ask myself. They are questions/dilemmas that top club coaches will have to resolve in their own circumstances. Mentioning them might imply criticism, but this section would not be complete if they were left out.

1. Could I have done more to help a captain?
Inevitably I didn't agree with all of the decisions made in the middle, but the harder part was to find a constructive dialogue, which actually helped matters. Once a game had started and we were in the field, I couldn't control what went on in the middle - and who bowled with what type of field to which opposition batter. Finding ways of being constructively critical and yet retaining a positive relationship is a diffi-

cult skill.

Reflection on the previous two successful seasons made me recognise that when I held a different view to that of the captain, I responded by trying to make his decisions work. I thought, in fact, that that was the appropriate role for a coach. It worked for two years largely though one-to-one discussion with players. In 2000, this strategy faltered and with hindsight, I should have had more assertive discussion with the captain.

2. Could I have had more influence on the selection committee?

I had chosen not to be a member of the selection committee, so in a sense felt the need to be diplomatic when selection didn't stimulate more competition for places. This poses the question: Should a coach be part of selection committee? Should a coach and captain determine their preferred team prior to selection?

3. Could I have had more influence in general club matters?

There was significant controversy within the club as to which team should represent the club in which league at 2ndteam level. The Premier Division 2nd XI competition and the Staffs Club Championship where most of the opposition had an overseas player were the options. The season started with the 2nd selected side playing in the Staffs Clubs Championship and the 3rd selected side in the Birmingham Premier 2nd XI competition. This proved a contentious issue and led to considerable disagreement and certainly created a divided club that didn't produce a climate in which difficulties could be easily resolved. Disaffection can spread quickly in such circumstances. I chose to regard my role as "coach - employee" and therefore didn't interfere with club politics, although it didn't stop me expressing concern about the affect it was having on players. The above account of an internal problem is perhaps parochial, but it represents the internal politics that most clubs experience in some way or other.

All of these three issues added up to a situation that meant that the art of coaching was made very difficult. For 2001, the third issue has been resolved, and I have come to the conclusion that I need to be more active in selection policies and to become even more active in coordinating strategy with the captain. Hopefully, with these issues clearer in my own mind, I will be able to focus on the identifiable coaching skills.

The success of 1998 and 1999 had meant that individual and team motivation and group dynamics had almost looked after itself. I now accept that I need a modified plan to ensure continued success, and not rely on success itself to keep us on the right track.

So even though this book is hopefully including good practice, it is not a definitive answer to the challenge of being a top club coach. All of us will have our unique set of difficulties to overcome. I am constantly developing my skills and no doubt you are doing the same otherwise you wouldn't be reading this book!

It only remains to conclude this chapter by referring to the pre-season strategy planned for the 2001 season. The strategy involved discussing the captain and vice-captains priorities in preparation for a team meeting some time in March. The meeting was brought forward from the normal March slot to February 12th, which is almost 11 weeks before the first league match, in order to give us more time to prepare.

Because the preparation for the 2001 season followed on from the disappointments of 2000, the process described in chapter 2 - "Preparation" was not only brought forward, but it was also structured in more detail. The captain, vice captain and coach were all agreed that a longer lead in to the season would be beneficial to the players.

It was now customary for me to assume that I bring the agenda, which was:

1.   To discuss the likely 1st team squad

2.   To analyse the strengths of that squad

    a. To look at batting in order to classify players who could perform the following roles:
      "Solid"
      "Strokemaker"
      "Match winner"
      "In tough situations"

    b. To look at bowling in order to classify players who could perform the following roles:
      "Strike"
      "Economical"
      "Consistent"
      "In tough situations"
      "Partnership breakers"

3.   To discuss the implications of the above analysis for strategy and tactics, and to discuss the need for clarity of role for players in the team.

4.   To look at the probable team and batting order
      To look at probable replacements when required
      To look at the probable bowling line up
      To look at probable replacements when required
      To look at wicket keeping and replacements

5.   To look at overall targets or team goals

6.   To discuss and agree the type of cricket we want to play and

develop the main strands of what will become "Team Performance Goals" after the full team meeting.

See the notes on the next two pages recording the outcome of the meeting in general terms. It was a record of a process of thinking of captain, vice captain and coach. It put the three of us in front in our planning, gave us all time to reflect of what had been discussed and would provide a strong resource to take to the 1st team squad meeting. It would be the 1st team squad meeting, however, that would finally determine our agreed overall team goals and team performance goals.

This agenda was then discussed with the chairman of selectors as a way of sounding out the approach. This received a positive response and so a 1st team squad meeting was arranged for March 19th to determine our priorities and performance targets for 2001. This was still almost 6 weeks before the first league match and left plenty of time to fine tune the planning.

The agenda was:

1. Club captain - (for whatever he wanted to say)

2. Chairman of selectors (again for whatever he wanted to say)

3. Coach - the main playing conditions for 2001

4. Coach - how the captain, vice captain and coach had agreed to work together during 2001, with particular reference to selection, practice and match preparation.

5. The players were placed in three groups as agreed between captain and coach. Captain, vice captain and coach, chaired a group each.

    a. Overall targets

       Position in league

       Approach to wins and defeats

    b. Our agreed priorities

    c. What type of cricket do we want to play?
       Performance targets for
       Fielding
       Bowling
       Batting
       Attitude

6. Availability for Easter weekend

7. Any other business

The outcome of the group discussions which led to report backs and summaries of opinion and further whole squad discussion were similar to those of the captain and vice captain recorded below. There was some difference of opinion, which is healthy, but there was also broad consensus as to how we should play with the resources that we had.

That's the preparation done. It's now a case of "Making Things Happen".

SETTING TARGETS

Approach to the season –Tim Heap (Captain) & Greg Wright (V.C.) – following an analysis of strengths. To be taken to team meeting and hopefully arrived at through discussion – not imposed. Likely to change shape and feature additions and deletions in final "Performance Goals" format.

OVERALL TARGETS

POSITION IN LEAGUE   TOP 5

WINS   To win every game we play until it becomes impossible. This demands judgement on part of Tim/Greg. Tim to express expectation in this area and the need for team responsibility.

DEFEATS   To become hard to beat

THE TYPE OF CRICKET WE WANT TO PLAY – Tim Heap and Greg Wright

OVERALL
* To play exciting entertaining cricket
* To impose ourselves on the opposition
* To do OUR thing & better than the opposition.

BATTING
* To be positive but this doesn't mean a shot a ball
* To take singles – every ball is a potential opportunity
* To make 1's into 2's and 2's into 3's
* To think 2's and 3's not 4's
* To rotate the strike and maintain a tick-over run rate
* To create partnerships
* To put the fielding side under pressure (They are generally older and poorer fielders and this needs to be exploited).

BOWLING
* To be positive but this doesn't mean a wicket a ball
* To bowl straight, off stump & bowl to field

- To 'not' strive for wickets as a main strategy or first priority
- To frustrate through maidens and low economy
- To make frequent bowling changes
- To show faith in all selected bowlers.

FIELDING

- To give it the "full works"
- To prevent opposition doing what is listed in "Batting above"
- To minimise mistakes
- To analyse performance (catches taken/dropped, quality takes/misfields runs saved/given away etc).

ATTITUDE OF TEAM

- To remind that the ghost of 2000 has been exorcised
- To remind that this is a new era
- To be positive even when the outcome is a draw
- To have a commitment to practice
- To have a commitment to timekeeping
- To have a commitment to pre-match warm-up
- To review performance after each match
- To warm down as a team whenever possible at the end of the game – fun activity.

OTHER

- To consider a sponsored or part sponsored polo top for everyone to arrive/wear, at beginning of a match.

There are four parts:
- General jogging/running to warm up the core body temperature
- Static stretching
- Ball skills
- Specific cricket skills: batting, bowling & wicket keeping, catching & ground fielding

This is one example of a warm up:

An area on the outfield is chosen to work in. For home matches this is the same area, as the routine associates the area used with the purpose – to warm up. For away matches, an area is chosen which is generally well away from the pavilion and close to shade (when available) if it is a hot sunny day.

The pre-prepared area to be worked in is marked with plastic mini cones in the form of a rectangular grid and set up as below. Separately, kwik cricket stumps are erected at the end of the square and another set just off the square for seam and spin bowlers to use at the end of the warm up.

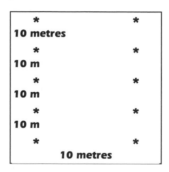

- The jogging warm up involves running around the outside of the cones, down the middle, zigzagging or a mixture. It would involve running forward, sideways and backwards. Zigzagging is particularly useful when moving sideways. When the muscles are warm, high knee raises, heel kicks, arm circles etc will be added and short sprint bursts at 50%, 75%, and 90% capacity for 10 metres.

- The players finish and make a large circle like a clock, in order that everyone can see each other – a "team" feel. Static stretches are then carried out for the neck, rear shoulder and trunk, shoulder and triceps, chest and shoulder, lower back and side, back and buttock, side, groin, quadriceps, hamstrings, achilles and calf, or sometimes in the reverse order as described in the ECB Manual on page 8.5. This would be followed by exercises to warm up the eyes as described in chapter 3 by either tracking my left and right hand alternately or switching between splice and top of mini bat handle when it is moved about.

- Ball skills are then added that are cricket related, e.g., underarm intercept and return to the wicket keeper and/or coach in two groups; catching in pairs followed by more advanced catching and fielding drills, with different skills introduced each week to keep things interesting.

• At this point, the final team talk/chat will often take place, but the timing of the chat needs to be right for the particular day.

• The final part of the warm up involves players working in groups according to their cricket specialism: seam bowlers bowl along the strip on the edge of the square to the wicket keeper; spin bowlers bowl to each other on the marked strip just off the edge of the square, fielders/batters choose to prioritise catching and ground fielding drills or batting in the net area with throw downs or sometimes both.

This then leaves at least 15 minutes for players to "chill out" and do whatever is best for them personally. Some listen to their headphones, others prefer conversation while others find a quiet space in which to focus their attention.

The ECB Manual lists the reasons for warming up, and when they are read, it's hard to see why any cricketer would be reluctant to warm up!

The warm up:
• Prepares the body for action by warming the muscles up and gradually increases heart rate;
• Increases range of movement;
• Improves co-ordination and aids skill development
• Improves bowling, throwing and running speed;
• Reduces the chance of injury and, improves performances.

I would add that, for the top club side, it also mentally warms up the team for the task ahead. That is why some of the ball skills are made mentally challenging.

Static stretching is the safest way to stretch muscles although there is increasing attention being paid towards dynamic stretching when the body is moving. Carefully handled, dynamic stretching can bring significant variation to warm ups, although the coach is strongly advised to be absolutely sure of what he/she is doing before undertaking them. The ECB Coach Development Workshop programme includes a short course on "Fitness and Training for Cricket Coaches" and the aspect of dynamic stretching is included. Separately, two systems exist ("SAQ" – Speed, agility and quickness, and "Speedtraining" from Adidas), but as their name suggests, they are more specific in objective. It is essential that the exercises be learned on an approved course however. Both alternatives can make a valuable contribution to the area of warming up.

The routine of warming up and stretching may take a while to set up, but once team performances improve, it will become a non-issue.

There are many ways of creating an interesting warm up. The coach needs to be always searching for ways to keep the players interested. The players will not warm up properly otherwise.

NATIONAL CLUB CHAMPIONSHIP FINAL
FRIDAY, 3rd SEPTEMBER 1999
Teddington v Wolverhampton

Itinerary for Thursday 2nd and Friday 3rd September:

Thursday 2nd September

10.00a.m.	Party staying at the Regent's Park Hilton leave Wolverhampton Cricket Club by coach.
12.30-1.00p.m.	Approximate time of arrival at the hotel.
1.30p.m.	*** Meet in hotel reception to either walk or take a very short coach ride to the W. G. Grace gates entrance to Lord's and take kit to dressing room 5. Smart casual dress.
2.00-4.00p.m.	*** Nets booked on the Nursery ground.
4.00p.m.	*** Return to hotel. Kit left in dressing room 5 overnight.
4.00-7.00p.m.	Free time.
7.00p.m.	Meet in hotel reception. Lounge suits or jacket and tie. Walk a few 100 yards to the Banqueting Suite at Lord's. Eve of final dinner 7.30p.m. for 8.00p.m.
10.00p.m.	Approximate time of return to hotel.

*** Assumes the Minor Counties MCC K.O. Trophy was completed on Wednesday. If it carries into Thursday then we would be able to watch it but not move our kit into dressing room 5. The groundsman also has to approve the conditions for practice if there is no match carryover.

Friday 3rd September

7.30a.m.	Breakfast (Full English booked unless requested otherwise)
8.15a.m.	Meet in hotel reception. Smart casual or jacket and tie. Room and breakfast is courtesy of the ECB. Any extras must be paid for when handing in keys and checking out.

CHAPTER FIVE

8.30a.m.	Short walk to Lord's taking overnight gear with us.
8.45a.m.	Captain and coach report team presence to ECB Competitions Manager, Mark Campkin, and the M. C. C. Duty Secretary
8.45-9.00a.m.	* Change into tracksuit bottoms or whites (no shorts allowed) for warm up on the nursery ground. Takes 8-10 minutes to walk from dressing room to nursery ground which is beyond the media centre.
9.15-10.10a.m.	* Warm up.
10.10a.m.	* Return to dressing room with kit.
10.25a.m.	* Approximate time for captains to toss up on the pitch. The allocated pitch will be number 5 or 6 in from the Mound Stand.
10.30a.m.	* Official photographs taken in the Coronation Gardens Turn right out of back of pavilion and the gardens are on the left.
11.00a.m.	Start of play
	Lunch will be taken between innings - 40 minutes
5.30-6.00p.m.	* Presentations followed by tea at the completion of the match.
7.00p.m.	* Private function at "Crocker's Folly", a pub about 5 minutes walk from the W. G. Grace gates. Kit taken with us.
9.30p.m.	Approximate time of departure by coach for Wolverhampton Cricket Club.
	* Times subject to variation

Players who want to stay overnight on Friday 3rd September will need to make their own arrangements and to take responsibility for getting to their Saturday League matches.

During the match, committee and friends will have tickets which will admit them to the pavilion. We will request that they do not come into the dressing room during the time that Wolverhampton are batting.

THE COACH : RISING TO THE CHALLENGE

Up to this point, chapters two, three and four have focussed on three things: that preparation is the heart of success, that the vital ingredients need to be integrated and that communication is the crucial factor. Putting it all together is the goal that chapter 5 attempted. This chapter now looks at "where is the coach coming from", "what makes the coach tick" and what is the background thinking that's been instrumental in what has been written in the earlier chapters.

The following areas will be looked at:

- Starting a coaching career - difficulties and all!
- The coaching philosophy that guides the practice?
- "Keeping all the balls in the air"
- The aims and objectives that give structure and clarity?
- Coaching style
- Uphill battles - Strategies for turning things round
- The coach and the press
- Formal relationships with a club
- "How to stay sane!"
- Meeting the needs of the coach
- Concluding thoughts

Starting a coaching career - difficulties and all!

The motives that draw coaches into coaching will vary considerably. The description that follows indicates one motive that might be appropriate for the experienced ex-player. It is personal but helps inform, "where I have been coming from" and what experiences have influenced what has been written.

It was a chance meeting during the autumn of 1997 and a subsequent discussion that led to me becoming coach of Wolverhampton Cricket Club in 1998. I was 54 at the time and looking ahead as to how to finish the love affair with the playing side of the game at top club level, and knew that it was not going to be the slow process of moving through the lower teams.

About a year earlier the National Cricket Association and the Test and County Cricket Board had published a National Development Plan for Cricket in "Towards the Millennium" in which the second objective was "To ensure a vibrant club game". The ECB after its formation on January 1st, 1997, had taken that objective further when it produced "Raising the Standard" in which a high priority was placed on the creation of Premier Leagues with an associated pyramid structure underpinning them. The ECB had a vision of giving the most talented club cricketers the opportunity to fulfil their potential by playing a format of the game more akin to First Class cricket alongside players contracted to First Class Counties.

Yes, that was it – I wanted to develop the talents of potentially top cricketers and where better to do it than at Wolverhampton Cricket Club where Arthur Pickering, following earlier work from Vic Mitchell, had since the mid 70's been developing a youth section which was now in 1998 very strong. The gap in the system, however, was that when players reached 17, they were "on their own", so to speak. The appointment of a coach for senior cricket appeared to be a possible answer in order to develop a seamless thread of development for all junior members.

Before we knew it I was asked to create my own terms of reference, as I was told, "I knew what was required"! See the end of this chapter for the terms of reference for 2000 and 2001. This has evolved and is the third version since joining the club.

Soon after starting at Wolverhampton Cricket Club it became clear that there was a massive gap between my expectations and that of the players. What I was asking for was a culture shock, especially on match days. I expected a level of commitment that was not forthcoming. Some players, for example, found the warm up an opportunity to "fool around" and the pre-match briefing all "a bit too serious", not to mention the late arrival of the same players. There was also a great deal of scepticism as to the need to eat and drink the right things before coming to the match and to top up both water and energy levels just before the match - the latter with bananas and chew bars.

The attitude of a few became unacceptable to me and I asked to see the committee about half way through the season to tell them that the club were wasting their money. The outcome was that we would give it a last try with the captain having a word with the players. The report included at the end of the chapter gives the flavour of the dilemma.

On the other hand I needed to reflect on what changes should be made to *my* approach. The conclusion was that more flexibility was required from me. Once the decision had been made to regard one senior player as a maverick and to publicly announce that we had negotiated that he was to be given licence to "do it his own way", and to another potentially loose cannon (also a senior player) to publicly announce that we had negotiated that he dispense with the formal warm-up but would be ready for the final part where bowlers needed a wicket keeper, things improved dramatically. The warm-ups with 9 players then became sharp, focussed and motivated. It wasn't ideal, but it's something that can happen when you become coach to an established side. Success is still possible!

Practice was also changed. Instead of looking after the first team squad, we opened up the evening practice session to the whole club membership over the age of 17. This was partly because it was proving impossible to get the whole first team squad together anyway, and partly because in terms of succession planning and promoting the players of the future, the culture change to attitudes towards practice could be gradually introduced and accepted. There is a long way to go, however, before we reach the accepted norm of say a top Australian Premier League side. The level of commitment required will only emerge as the younger players come through with a different culture of expectation.

The report mentioned above is included (at the end of the chapter) to indicate that a coach should not underestimate the culture change that is required and that hard work will be needed to change attitudes. Success is however, attainable and attitudes can be changed. Further progress has been made at Wolverhampton over the last winter, and the players have committed themselves to regular practice following the disappointments of the 2000 season and have agreed that attendance at practice should be a factor in selection criteria. To succeed overall however, the coach needs to think long-term and to be patient, flexible, realistic and pragmatic.

The description above relates to an ex-player who made coaching a second career. At the other end of the spectrum, there is great opportunity for the younger person to make coaching cricket a career. It will require hard work and, in my opinion, the ECB Level I, II and III coaching awards will be essential. For this person, the book is intended to assist the process of choosing whether coaching cricket as a career is appropriate for them.

There is also plenty of room for the coach of a top club side who has another job during the week. It just means that effective time management will be a major requirement.

The coaching philosophy that guides the practice

If a coach is to have a sense of purpose, then I believe that they need a vision of what it is they are trying to achieve. This implies that they have a philosophy that drives the way they coach. It doesn't necessarily need to be written down, but the coach should be able to explain what drives him/her on. *My personal philosophy has developed over many years and can be found at the end of this chapter.* It isn't set in concrete and could well be modified in the light of experience. It is a very personal document, but I share it in the spirit in which the book is being written.

The word "I" is used a lot in this section because it couldn't be avoided. It's because the section is personal and largely concerned with opinion. As a coach, I know I perform several roles of which the following are five of the most important: leader, organiser, communicator, manager and guardian of values.

To lead well, I need integrity, dependability and positive direction. To organise I need to be well prepared, thorough and to anticipate. To communicate I need to possess both verbal and non-verbal skills. To manage I need to be sensitive to the needs of others. And to be a guardian of values, I need to have a vision as to what I mean when I use the words quality, improvement and standards, and to embrace the concept of equal opportunities in everything I do. Guardian of values also embraces the "Spirit of the Game".

This implies an ethical approach to coaching. The ECB in its manual suggest guidelines that are designed to ensure that coaches "behave in a professional way and hence avoid any complaints regarding their personal behaviour, competence or conduct". The ECB also expect coaches to follow a code of conduct "which reflect credit on them and the whole process and practice of cricket coaching".

The ECB highlight issues such as relationships, commitment, integrity, confidentiality and safety, as well as the important issues of child protection. Child protection, which includes consideration of child abuse, is an essential part of as Level I Coaching Award, while emergency "Life Support" is an essential part of a Level II Coaching Award. (There is a compulsory written assessment for "Child Abuse" and a compulsory attendance requirement and assessment for "Life Support" unless there is evidence of prior learning.)

I think it is our duty as coaches to uphold the ECB "Code of Conduct and Spirit of Cricket" document for players that can be found in the "Regulations and Playing Conditions for Non First Class Competitions" which is produced each year in handy pocket size. This document includes the words "The Captains are responsible at all times for ensuring that play is conducted within that Spirit of the Game as well is within the Laws", and I believe it essential that the coach supports this objective even if there are the occasional disagreements. Debate on these issues is essential if the more recent trends at International level are to be minimised at club level.

The final inclusion at the end of the chapter is another source of information about standards. It can be found in the National Coaching Foundation's "Coaches' Charter". This includes the important issue of ensuring equal opportunities for all those who wish to participate in the game. It is important, I believe, that coaches take on the responsibility for the promotion of the game with players irrespective of their gender, race, creed or social circumstance.

I would like to leave you with two final thoughts in this section on philosophy. Within the context of our responsibility to coach with a 'Duty of Care' for the people we coach, and irrespective of the result of any one particular match, I like to think that it's the journey and not just the destination that is important, and that success for a coach is improvement in performance.

"Keeping all the balls in the air"

The top club coach has a wide number of elements that he/she needs to consider. In trying to visualise a way of representing them, I first came up with the carpet weave effect which was a two-dimensional model. Diagram 1 below represents this carpet weave effect. It shouldn't matter which strand of the carpet that the coach begins by focusing upon; the perceptive coach will understand how the strand relates to all the other strands.

There were the five ingredients of physical, mental, technical, tactical and lifestyle components, and each of these were applied to the coaching skills required of a coach in batting, pace bowling, spin bowling, wicket keeping and fielding.

On reflection the two-dimensional approach didn't appear to cover all the elements that needed to be considered. Therefore I came up with a three-dimensional model that also included safety, child protection, gender, ethnicity, disability, deprivation, improvement, standards and fun and enjoyment, as well as the two dimensions that the ECB use in the Level III course: interpersonal and management skills. See diagram 2 over.

Diagram 1

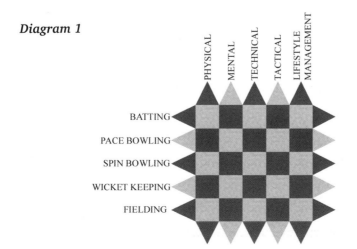

Diagram2

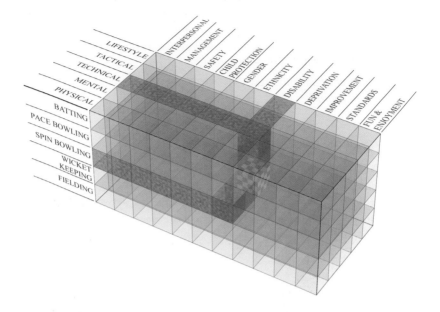

The top club coach will be attempting to "keep all the balls in the air" and to be developing the skill to enter the cube from any direction and to see the inter-relationships.

I visualise this whole diagram as similar to a box of sugar cubes. Enter the box from any of the three dimensions, and there will be only one sugar cube where all three meet. In the above example, the "chequered sugar cube" is when 'spin bowling', 'technical' and 'disability' meet. If my maths is correct, there are 275 "sugar cubes" available! Understanding where each cube is situated is a tough task for the coach. Perhaps it is a goal to strive towards.

The aims and objectives that give structure and clarity

This title does not refer to the goals and performance targets of a team, but to the aims and objectives of the individual coach. These aims and objectives are in the context and recognition that top club cricket is not a professional game, even though there is more money at this level than there used to be in the form of travel expenses and payment.

While I, like the team, want to win things, this isn't the motivation for my aims and objectives. I believe that if the aims and objectives are appropriate, then winning becomes a much more likely bi-product that fits in with developing performance philosophy. The following aims are listed for consideration:

- To maximise the potential of the team/squad
- To provide a seamless thread of development for younger players
- To strive for agreed minimum standards
- To strive for the team performance which could be called the perfect game
- To communicate to the team/squad a belief that quality cricket produces quality results
- To try to bridge the gap between top club cricket and the professional game.

The above could be described as aims. They are the broad-brush strokes of what it is a coach is trying to achieve.

I believe that after determining the overall aims, the coach needs to then break this into more specific and manageable chunks or objectives. The real skill for the coach is the decision making process of determining what the next step of development is for a particular team/squad. Hopefully the contents of this book will give plenty of inspiration in this area and that once broad-brush aims have been determined, the objectives can be formulated in a gradual and logical sequence. Everything can't be done at the same moment. The coach needs to prioritise and take one step at a time. Recognise that it takes time to implement changes and seek evolution rather than revolution.

As an example, I refer to the fact that it has taken Wolverhampton three years, before it has been agreed that the team are ready to move onto the creation of performance targets as described at the end of chapter 5. These performance targets will provide a benchmark by which we can judge our playing standards. It's another step forward.

Although this section is brief, its importance should not be underestimated.

Coaching Style

The majority of what needs to be said has already been said in other parts of the book. The introduction encouraged coaches to be positive; to be different and to be you and this will undoubtedly be the most important factor in determining coaching style. The early part of chapter four distinguishes between alternative styles of communication, while later in the same chapter in the section on 'Match play and the team' the difference between, for example, words like training on the one hand and empowerment on the other is expanded upon. Coaching style is all about chosen communication methods and about varying one's approach according to the ability, maturity and experience of the player.

Whatever the coaching style used, the successful coach will have to have enthusiasm and commitment. In addition I think they will have to be true to themselves, to care for the people they coach and to be efficient and flexible. This flexibility is vital if the coach is to make the best and most imaginative use of every opportunity that arises.

Finally, in this short section, coaches are urged to remember that they can't do it on their own, and that time needs to be found to maintain positive relationships with a wide spectrum of people including club members, officials, helpers and employees as well as the players. The 'Personal philosophy of cricket coaching' at the end of this chapter emphasises this point.

Uphill battles - Strategies for turning things round

Success is its own motivator. The real challenge for the coach is when things are going wrong. There are no magic formulas, only graft, hard work, more hard work, instilling self-belief in the team and having realistic expectations

Situations at top club level vary and uphill battles can be due to:

- Depleted resources through unavailability for such things as weddings, holidays and county representative selection
- Depleted resources through injury
- Limited resources within the team or squad
- Inexperience at coping with particular climatic or pitch conditions
- Underachievement by the team.

There are no easy answers. Perhaps the following strategies can help.

Short term

- Look for positives in the previous performance(s)
- Emphasise the control of the controllable
- Review the clarity with which the roles of individual players, within a given match situation, have been communicated
- Be more specific about what you want from the batter, the bowler etc.
- Set up specific practices to mitigate against shortcomings on specific pitches such as young players adapting to slow and low pitches in April

- Go for the quiet vibes of simplicity

– Batters take one ball at a time and play each ball on its merit

– Bowlers put the ball in the right places and be specific if necessary

– Wicket keepers and fielders - one ball at a time and its coming to you

- Use all avenues of communication - individual, pairs, groups and team

- Work on raising players expectations of themselves so that they play to a higher level than they thought possible

- Be realistic - the return may not be in proportion to the effort you put in

- Avoid panic - your anxiety will spread to the team

    (See chapter 5 for more specific ideas.)

Longer term

- Look to strengthening the squad in depth if uncontrollable factors concerning unavailability and injury lead to inequality in the contest with the opposition

- Consider goal setting for both team and individuals

- Consider performance goals for how the team believe they should play in order to have a benchmark for measuring performance.

    (See earlier in this chapter and in chapters 4 and 5.)

The coach and the press

Despite the wide-ranging nature of what has been included, there are still other areas of expectation for the coach. The particular area I am thinking of is the media and in particular the local press. The coach needs to develop relationships, which clearly understand when a comment is "off the record" or "on the record". I recommend that the journalists with whom you co-operate accept this division as a condition of dialogue. And even then, it is important to choose your words carefully.

Carefully worded comment can boost the confidence of the team in the same way as careless language can do a lot of damage to team morale. And in individual terms, sometimes when a player has done particularly well after a lean time, a proactive 'phone call can ensure the confidence boosting exposure for a particular player. Because the telephone frequently rings to ask for information, I make a few notes and am ready when the time comes. In this way I try to influence the angle the press take. If I am not proactive, it is far more likely that the press will interpret matters in a different way. Give them a story and they are less likely to make one up.

The key rule is to have the information at your fingertips so that what is quoted is accurate. There is nothing more annoying for the players than to be wrongly reported. Work with the captain as well to ensure that your experience is available in order to reduce the inevitable pitfalls that exist whenever the press are involved.

Formal relationships with a club

If a coach wants to become a top club coach then I recommend the following route:

- Obtain the ECB qualifications already recommended. Remember an ECB Level III award is a very powerful tool.

- Compile cricket curriculum vitae in readiness.

- Clarify what you think you can do for the club involved, because they will certainly ask you. Have a strategy prepared as to where you would start.

- Carry out your homework in order that you know what other support coaches exist and an answer as to how you would work with them

- Keep your ear close to the ground for any grapevine information re opportunities

- Ensure that you will be working to a job description and terms of reference

"How to stay sane!"

There was a section in chapter 4 on "Control the Controllable" when applied to practice and the team, and it is equally important for the coach to remember the same thing when it applies to him/herself.

However hard the coach works, there are decisions which will be out of his/her control. There is only one captain once the team enter the field of play. The coach can talk about bowling strategies and field placing, but once the team have left the pavilion it is the captain who will change the bowling and set the field. Similarly, whatever planning has gone into individual, pairs, group or team discussion, once the batters are in the middle, it is they who will decide what shots to play, and once the ball is in the hand of the bowler, the coach cannot control it.

The coach needs to be able to identify what is controllable and uncontrollable. It helps to recognise that sometimes when things are going well the uncontrollable "breaks" are with you. If this is recognised when things are going well for the team, it makes it easier to cope when the "breaks" are going against the team. Hang onto this - it will help to keep you sane!

"Meeting the needs of the coach"

This is closely related to "How to stay sane" and contributes to the same end. It can refer to both the personal and the professional life of the coach.

A friend or a partner can frequently meet the needs of a coach. We individually solve most of our problems in life, but talking to a good listener often speeds up the process. The support of a friend or partner can also maintain the coach's morale. Coach's, like players, need encouragement and praise.

One example of friendly encouragement occurred on the day on the National Club Championship Final at Lord's in 1999. All my energy was being poured into the needs of the team, and so it was great to receive the following text message on my mobile.

"Hope my very best wishes help u today. Stay strong. Concentrate on the +ve. Stay focussed and most importantly ENJOY". The same person was able to receive mobile 'phone calls both on that day and on other occasions when talk helped to maintain calm in some tense match situations.

If you coach, and also enjoy playing, then try to leave space for playing. Commitment to coaching doesn't mean that you have to stop playing although match play will be inevitably reduced. And always take your kit to matches as if you were a 12th man, unless of course you are a player coach in the first place! In every year so far, some emergency has arisen that has necessitated me taking the field!

Professionally, I think that the coach should always be striving to improve. It was mentioned earlier that a commitment to personal development is important if the standard of coaching is to rise. It was also mentioned in chapter 2 that my own planning for practice, for example, was always looking for ways to improve, and this is true of every aspect of my coaching. If I come across a good idea, I'll use it. It doesn't matter who makes the suggestion from the most experienced to the least experienced. What matters is the quality of the suggestion. Motivating a team depends on keeping things fresh, so although the messages might be very similar, the "parcel" (message) has to be wrapped in many different styles of wrapping paper. This book has frequently, by implication, recommended the ECB Coaching Awards Scheme, and success in cess in this area is the vehicle to very important update information and in-service training opportunities.

In January 2002, membership of the Association of Cricket Coaches will transfer into the ECB Coaches Association. There will be no better way of staying in touch than to transfer/join this new association and to also apply for a licence to coach. Licences will expect a commitment to in-service training and the ECB will make in-service opportunities available.

Every year there will be an opportunity to attend a conference. The ECB Performance Department organise Cricket Live, the World Cricket Coaches Conference and Exhibition, and this will alternate with County or where appropriate, Regional conferences. In addition, the coaching award scheme, which rises vertically from Level I to Level V with levels I - III being the most likely for the top club coach, will be supplemented by courses targeted horizontally for those coaches who want to become more proficient at their present level or inclined for those coaches who wish to prepare for the next level (see diagram on page 39).

In addition, an excellent ECB publication called "Hitting the Seam" makes sure that coaches know what's going on. Together the conferences, courses and literature are a positive investment in personal advancement.

Finally, when thinking about yourself, remember, just like performers, you need rest and the opportunity to recharge your own batteries.

Concluding thoughts

- Frank Dick in 9 words in his presentation to "Cricket Live" in 1999 (7) said so much that summarised what I feel about coaching. I agree with him totally when he says of the coach that it his/her job to provide "the roots to grow and the wings to fly".

- The coaches involved with a player at the beginning of their cricketing life will be concerned with the important first "roots", but progress can be impeded however, if a coach promotes a dependency culture. At each stage players need to be given increasing responsibility for their own game.

- At top club level as players become increasingly mature in both personal and cricketing terms, it is the "wings to fly" that is far more appropriate. Again an analogy from Frank Dick in the same presentation describes it perfectly. The coach needs to be the "wind beneath the wings". Players need to become as self sufficient as possible at this level. Our job is to 'empower' the players to take control.

- Each day a coach should be striving to be a better coach than the previous day. This may be due to a cricketing experience or just something that happens in daily life.

- As in life, the coach needs to accept that there will be 'ups' and 'downs' and that both need to be accepted with good grace

- Part of the fun of coaching is the challenge - the mountains to climb

- The picture and caption below says it all in the photograph taken after Wolverhampton won the National Club Championship at Lords on Friday 3rd September 1999.

"The reward"

If a coach is on the photograph it implies that he/she was important, but to say that the coach is important is to deflect the credit away from the players.

To deflect the credit away from the players doesn't build for tomorrow and doesn't give the team the "wings to fly" to use Frank Dick's phrase. (7)

If the one-to-one work of the coach is effective, only the coach knows the collective whole.

The future performance and self-belief of the team depends significantly on the players believing that they largely did it themselves.

In my opinion, the true art of the coach is to help create within the team/squad that feeling of ownership over their own destiny. Over time the coach makes him/herself increasingly superfluous to requirements with the first team squad at top club level leaving the way clear to concentrate on working with players who will be part of a clubs future. I call this a "succession planning" policy.

WOLVERHAMPTON CRICKET CLUB

TERMS OF REFERENCE FOR 1ST XI CLUB COACH

1) To be directly responsible to the Club Captain. The Club Captain will pass all reports from the Club Coach to the General Management Committee. However, the Club Captain may invite the Club Coach to attend a General management Committee meeting when deemed appropriate.

2) To be responsible for organising, running and providing coaching at senior nets on Thursday night, (2 hour session – 6.00p.m. to 8.00p.m.) for all playing members over the age of 17.

3) To establish informal relationships with the Junior Section Coaches, in order to identify players with the potential of becoming 1st XI players of the future, especially those over 14 years of age. Ensuring that the Junior Chairman, Arthur Pickering, is kept in the communication loop.

4) To take a development interest in all senior players including those outside the XI squad.

5) To develop in collaboration with the 1st XI Captain and Vice Captain:
   a) An analysis of the 1st XI squad strengths and weaknesses leading to an agreed team strategy
   b) A systematic approach to analysing the strengths and weaknesses of the opposition and their likely strategy towards Wolverhampton.

6) To develop the natural talent of all 1st XI squad players by following the priorities of:
   a) Mental fitness/approach
   b) Understanding of the game
   c) Individual and team technique
   d) Physical fitness

7) To commit to the organisation of the pre-match warm up, individual counselling during the game, and making a contribution to a short end of match debrief, for all Birmingham & District Premier League games.

8) The Club Coach will be permitted to play on Sundays, in order to promote development of the young players, on a social membership plus match fee basis.

9) Specific details of the contractual and financial side of this role are included under the heading of "Personal Contract" and have been drawn up and agreed between the Club Coach, Club Captain and Club Chairman.

WOLVERHAMPTON CRICKET CLUB

PERSONAL CONTRACT

1) This contract is between John Moore, known hereafter as the CLUB COACH and Wolverhampton Cricket Club, known hereafter as THE CLUB

2) THE CLUB offers the CLUB COACH a contract of employment, with the terms of reference outlined in the attached document, for two cricketing seasons, beginning April 200? and expiring after September 200? cricket season.

3) A review of the duration of this contract, between the CLUB COACH and THE CLUB, can take place at any time within the originally agreed contract period. The purpose of this is in order to facilitate an agreement to extend this contract beyond the two years, should both parties agree.

4) THE CLUB agrees to release the CLUB C OACH from this contract only if he receives a formal offer from the ECB (English and Wales Cricket Board). The CLUB COACH agrees to hold no other negotiations with any other cricket club or move to any other cricket club during his contracted period with THE CLUB.

5) THE CLUB agrees to permit the CLUB COACH to act on a consultancy basis with any other cricket club or organisation, provided that this neither affects his agreed duties with THE CLUB nor that any inside knowledge about THE CLUB and its players are divulged.

6) THE CLUB agrees to permit the CLUB COACH to utilise the facilities at THE CLUB for private coaching sessions on an occasional basis and subject to availability.

7) THE CLUB agrees to the CLUB COACH increasing his income through personal sponsorship. Where this sponsorship involves THE CLUB and or its facilities, the CLUB COACH agrees to ensure that THE CLUB gains financially.

8) The presence of the CLUB COACH at matches relates to Saturday League games plus two Bank Holidays matches only.

9) THE CLUB and the CLUB COACH have agreed a two year fully inclusive of all expenses fee of £   . This fee is to be paid in two instalments each year: on the 11th and the 22nd Birmingham & District Premier League games.

REPORT TO WOLVERHAMPTON CRICKET CLUB

THURSDAY 2ND JULY 1998

Edited version which indicates the challenge of changing a culture within a club.

I had a vision of the future, gave up my Saturday playing career even though still capable of playing to a high level, and took on the job of 1st team coach, all of which seems to indicate a considerable commitment.

The vision was for Wolverhampton Cricket Club to become the premier club in the Midlands and for the first team to be the top team.

I created terms of reference, which were approved by the Club Captain, designed to ensure that the first team became secure in the Birmingham Premier League. I've kept to them.

In the pre-season meeting of Club Captain, 1st XI captain and vice captain and senior players we talked about priorities. We talked about the need for practice and to relate this to other knock out competitions. Application, dedication and commitment were expected from the team squad.

No names will be mentioned during the report that follows, as principles are the important issues not personalities. In my opinion, if the principles are clear, most of the personality issues resolve themselves.

PRACTICE

From the squad of 28, two are ignored – two contracted players.

There have been 10 practices (Attendance statistics were then quoted to indicate an unacceptably low figure.)

There are some mitigating circumstances such as work, exams, county matches and illness but it is things like knock out matches that have seriously undermined the agreed practice night.

LEAGUE MATCHES

Preparation is significant with an analysis of the opposition's recent performance, prior to the match. (And then an example was given.)

Timekeeping It was agreed with the captain that we should arrive and be changed to leave 1 hour for warm up and pre-match tactical preparation. This does not happen. (Examples were then given) Lateness is commonplace on the part of a significant number of players. It's a waste of time 6, 7 or 8 coming on time if a regular 3, 4 or 5 do not.

Warm ups I've tried to make them interesting, but have become increasingly frustrated at the way in which some players have made them into a joke. There is room for humour and fun, vital ingredients for a team's success, but it has to be within a context of commitment. Warm ups are also of limited value if not performed by all the team, because they act as a mental focus for the task in hand as well as helping to prevent injury.

Pre-match personal preparation I have stresses the importance when playing

55 overs in a 3 hours 20 minute non-stop session on nutrition and dehydration. Players are advised to eat a high carbohydrate meal two/three hours before the match and to top this up with bananas and chew bars just prior to the game.

Players are advised to drink one/two litres of water before travelling to the match and to top this up just prior to and during the game in order to prevent dehydration. Both energy supply and dehydration are regarded as important factors in maintaining top-level performance over an extended period of time. I have provided the bananas, chew bars and water, while very few players have provided their own.

Attitude Some players share my enthusiasm for the modern way of playing the game, but others don't appear to want to know. They argue that they work all week and appear to want fun and a laugh at the weekend. (The fact that other countries also work all week but show total commitment on Saturdays appears to escape their notice.) One player has played on two occasions out of the last four Saturdays quite obviously suffering from the previous nights alcohol intake.

CONCLUSIONS were then drawn and **RECOMMENDATIONS** made.

The report was ended with what I called **THE ESSENTIAL DILEMMA:**

With the exception of one younger player, the support of the under 25 age group has been positive.

It is in effect "too late" for four senior players to obtain major benefits from the modern way of doing things. And yet, they are important to the success of the team.

A code of expectation would encourage the senior players to decide which way to go. If this were out, then the consequence would be a younger and less experienced side.

Too few players are prepared to "work at it". Their collective application and commitment is too low for top sport.

Too few players understand that practice needs to have intensity for it to be effective.

The priorities of the club are unclear.

Does the club want to embrace the culture change that is required to become the best?

Can the senior players outside the first team come to terms with the need for the younger players, who provide less income for the club, to be an integral part of the longer-term future of the club?

Are the players prepared to apply themselves sufficiently to develop both their own and the teams talents?

Note: Despite the comments made in this report. It was after this report that the team ethic improved, with compromises made by both the coach and the players. The second half of the season improved dramatically in the areas referred to and subsequently led to the winning of the Inaugural Birmingham and District Premier Cricket League!

A PERSONAL PHILOSOPHY OF CRICKET COACHING

The philosophy is relatively simple. The cornerstone is a respect for the individual irrespective of his/her role. It applies equally to all those who contribute: to players of all ages, their parents where appropriate, other coaches, umpires, officials, ground staff, bar and refreshment staff/volunteers, supporters, and to any others who contribute to the game of cricket.

I believe that the way people treat each other has a major effect on our central purpose which is to ensure that the people we coach are given the maximum opportunity to develop their abilities and to achieve as much of their potential as possible. This includes encouraging the coached to become as self-sufficient as possible.

It is essential that coaches recognise that all those who receive coaching are of equal value and justify the same high standard of care and concern. There can be no room for discrimination. To dismiss a player as not being worthy of commitment creates a climate that leads to disillusionment and apathy, instead of a positive climate of optimism and co-operation.

All those we coach need to be stimulated by an active, challenging, demanding and supportive environment in which high expectations are made. I believe coaches who find excuses for the lack of success of the coached by blaming external factors are failing them.

Professionalism demands that we must aim high and never cease to increase our expectations of the coached. In order to achieve this, communication between coach and coached is vital to success. It must reflect and attribute a dignity to the coached, which coaches would want for themselves or a member of their family.

Would you settle for a coach who didn't prepare their sessions? Or who allowed the coached to do their own thing or does not seek to motivate them? Or who disregarded ECB or club directives, guidelines or codes of conduct? Or who is persistently late? Or who abuses by either deed of word? Or who constantly finds fault and rarely praises?

Everyone responds to having his or her efforts recognised, to being praised, to being encouraged, to being spoken to in a civil manner and to being constructively criticised.

To expect blind obedience from the coached does not square with respect for the individual. Being prepared to listen is all-important, but this does not mean that firm action is never taken. What matters, is that it is in the context of a warm, and caring relationship. If the coached believe that we care for them, faults and all, the vast majority will respond to a consistent, fair and structured coaching environment.

To be treated as professional in the management of our coaching, entails a degree of individual freedom, but it also demands responsibility - to have one without the other is an unequal and unacceptable formula.

In order to offer the very best to those being coached, we need to strive for greater expertise and this implies a commitment to personal development.

Coaches also need to be clear as to the values that underpin their coaching. I believe that we need to place greater emphasis on enjoyment being the by-product of quality cricket. This implies less emphasis on words like winning or losing or success or failure. Quality cricket produces successful winners who do not need to resort to gamesmanship and cheating, although the realities of the modern game played at top level cannot be totally ignored. Coaches, I believe, should also encourage inventiveness and originality.

The contribution to the attainment of the coach's aims of the non-playing members of the wider team should not be underestimated. Coaches depend on their support like the coached depend on the coach to achieve their potential. Collectively they contribute to club and team spirit and foster values where everyone involved is interested in the success of each other, and where, for example, pride in appearance and assisting with essential tasks without being asked, is important

The philosophy outlined referred to the achievement of the coached, the learning environment, expectations, discipline, communication, professional standards, personal development, management, values and the ways in which all those outside the coaching relationship can contribute to overall success.

My vision is where all coaches strive to create an environment in which the coached achieve their true potential and all those in the process gain satisfaction and self-fulfilment. It implies a commitment from all those within the structure to a similar philosophy.

Concern for the individual is paramount in an environment in which everyone involved has an equal right to be treated with dignity and respect.

THE COACHES' CHARTER

NATIONAL COACHING FOUNDATION

1. Coaches must respect the rights, dignity and worth of every person and treat everyone equally within the context of their sport.

2. Coaches must place the well-being and safety of the performer above the development of performance. They should follow all guidelines laid down by the sports governing body and hold appropriate insurance cover.

3. Coaches must develop an appropriate working relationship with performers (especially children), based on mutual trust and respect. Coaches must not exert undue influence to obtain personal benefit or reward.

4. Coaches must encourage and guide performers to accept responsibility for their own behaviour and performance.

5. Coaches should hold up-to-date and nationally recognised governing body coaching qualifications.

6. Coaches must ensure the activities they direct or advocate are appropriate for the age, maturity, experience and ability of the individual.

7. Coaches should at the outset clarify with performers (and where appropriate their parents) exactly what is expected of them and what performers are entitled to expect from their coach. A simple contract or agreed checklist may sometimes be appropriate.

8. Coaches should co-operate fully with other specialists (eg other coaches, officials, sports scientists, doctors, physiotherapists) in the best interests of the performer.

9. Coaches should always promote the positive aspects of their sport (eg fair play) and never condone rule violation or the use of prohibited substances.

10. Coaches must consistently display high standards of behaviour and appearance.

WHERE NEXT? LOOKING AHEAD

There is an element of crystal ball gazing in this brief chapter as the future of top club cricket is contemplated. It will be short, to the point and in the same style as the introduction.

The coaching of top club cricket is beginning to improve as more and more clubs take the step to appoint a coach. In the Birmingham & District Premier Cricket League in 1998, for example, Wolverhampton was the first club to make such an appointment. Since then other clubs have followed this lead with the appointment of coaches, managers or coach/managers, and not only at premier league level. This is beginning to make an impact on top club cricket, while promotion and relegation is also contributing to an improvement in standards. I anticipate that this improvement will continue as clubs realise that their top-level status will only be maintained through hard work. I think the 'penny has dropped'.

Modern digital technology has over the last few years opened up possibilities in video analysis at modest cost that has brought it within the reach of most coaches. This has been through personal, club or coaches association purchase. Expertise in its use is growing and the emphasis is now clearly on celebrating what is good about a person's game before looking at what can be improved.

Where video recording is used, the top club coach currently employs it as part of a process designed to improve the performance of his/her own players. Its use however, is currently limited by practical considerations and is frequently, but not exclusively, confined to indoor opportunities.

As technology from the first class game develops, I believe it is only a matter of time before it becomes available to top clubs. Some of the technology that is being used on television and with some first class counties is very impressive. When some of this technology becomes available to clubs, the analysis of both the home team and the opposition can be taken to new levels.

Television has introduced cameras that are square of the wicket and other angles to interest the viewer including inside the stump. There has been the advent of the "snickometers" to detect the cause of different sounds and "see through" imposed lines and circles to predict the "flight path" of the ball after it has, for example, hit the pad.

The television technology however that is more useful to the coach comes in two forms: the "super slowmo" and "split screen" techniques. The first, for example, can illustrate the difference between the leg break, the topspin, the googly and the flipper, while the second enables comparative performance analysis. Both can assist with specific technical analysis and the "Quintic" system below offers a similar facility but with more tricks!

As far back as the 1980's there was innovation in the use of computers to help strive for the ever increasingly small margins that make the difference between performers and teams. I was aware of a system that was used in Australia called CATCCH (Computer Aid to Cricket Coaching) that developed a game charting and analysis system, which focussed on how runs were accumulated and wickets taken.

The video analysis systems that I am aware of are "Crickstat", "Statsmaster", "Sportscode" and "Quintic". They are all targeted at top coaching levels.

"Crickstat" is a system devised in South Africa, which uses digital video processing and a special notational analysis. Two majors counties in England use it to my knowledge. An operator linked to cameras situated behind the wickets can log individual deliveries, which can be analysed on demand for specific players. For example a coach can recall instantly a batters entire innings in a short period of time because the spaces between deliveries are removed. Alternatively it can recall all the deliveries faced from a particular bowler. The other way round, the system can recall the bowler's entire contribution and further subdivide this into bowling to particular batters.

It is possible to 'search' for all "back foot shots" or all "googlies" etc. Wagon wheels can be constructed to indicate where batters score runs or in what areas of the field bowlers are more expensive than others. It works to an existing flexible template and can instantly recall in detail the consolidated record for review of whatever the coach has requested.

It saves time if the analysis is carried out while the game is in progress, but the analysis can be done after the event in what is called 'lapsed time'. The process can consolidate real time match play into a VHS tape that requires a quarter of the time to watch. E.g. 4 hours of match play can be viewed in 1 hour.

This can therefore not only be used to assist the technical development of each player's game, but also makes tactical analysis of opposition faults possible. It can also be used in a very positive way to record in a short version a quality innings or bowling spell from a particular player who, when it has been converted to VHS tape, can use it as a means of supporting positive thinking when confidence is perhaps in need of a boost.

The England team uses the "Statsmaster" system for both home and away matches. There is a performance analyst who watches every game. The analysis is carried out at the ground for home matches and via television coverage for away matches. The results of the latter can then be sent to the team via email.

This system also works to set but flexible parameters and can also be used for 'real' time or 'lapsed' time analysis. "Crickstat" and "Statsmaster" are both IBM compatible, and have a number of common features.

"Sportscode" is an Apple Mac system than can again 'save' specific parts of the game e.g. 'bowling to left handed batters'. The England Women's team, and the England Under 19's and 17's have all used it and it was introduced to the England regional under 15's, 14's and 13's in 2001.

One difference with "Sportscode" is that the coach can set up his/her own template. It's a matter of identifying what it is that the coach wants to record and then having the facility to isolate and compile a consolidated record to view.

The "Quintic" system is specifically designed to emphasise biomechanical analysis. The ECB National Coaches each have the system as too do a number of first class counties. It permits video analysis from a source level of the domestic digital video camera upwards and allows split screen technology to make comparisons between similar shots or bowling actions/deliveries.

As the technology becomes cheaper and more readily available, I can see it coming into selective use at top club level although the full-time analyst might only be possible if there is someone who wants to make it a retirement hobby! I also believe that the analysis of fielding and wicket keeping will become more prominent.

There are also hand held palm top computers being developed specifically for coaches that can be used for recording information during matches. And in the future I would be very surprised if technology didn't produce virtual reality simulators for cricket in the same way as pilots use simulators when learning to fly. Short of that I envisage, in addition to more advanced digital cameras, an increase in interactive CD's and DVD alternatives and greater use of the Internet for background information and interactive opportunities.

The scorebook colour coding referred to in chapter 3 in the section on 'tactical' seems to be like living in the 'dark ages' in comparison to modern technology even though it gives more information than just how many runs were scored and wickets taken. It also indicates which bowler bowled to which batter with what outcome. That however, is scratching the surface in terms of the information that would be beneficial to the coach.

I can see the advent of not only more electronic scoreboards at club level but also laptop computer scorebooks. The time that is saved through this method would enable more detailed "tracking" of such things as where shots have been played and how many runs scored, and for this through computer programmes to be made available at the press of a button to a coach. If some scorers have the expertise to not only score, but also compile flow charts and wagon wheels now, then just imagine what they could do with new technology! Maybe even aspects of the above systems could be introduced into laptop computer scorebooks.

The digital technology of video analysis and laptop scoring may seem a long way away from the club game, but I expect to see it while I am still an active coach!

Irrespective of the technology mentioned above, I think the game is ripe for new invention. In recent years there have been new ways developed for both wrist spin and finger spin bowlers. There have been new shots developed; especially for the one-day game while tactics have developed to much more sophisticated levels to combat opposition strengths. Policies change over preferred styles of play. Australia have led the way with their positive approach to the game while England are showing that they have what it takes to live at the very highest level. Competition is becoming tougher and more demanding of players. I have no problem with that as long as we preserve the spirit and integrity of the game within the context of using every available resource to improve the quality of performance.

This book has ambitiously attempted to:

• Indicate where you might start

• Focus on forward planning

• Share practical ideas

• Trigger new thinking

• Link together the major factors

• Give strategies for making things happen

• Look at prioritising

• Build strong foundations for future development

• Promote the ECB coaching scheme

If this book had been written at the end of the 2001 season, it would have been better, and so it should have been. In the same way, if what we are doing in five years time is the same as now, then that I regard as standing still and going backwards in relative terms.

Coaching will play a vital role in the attainment of the ECB vision "to become and remain the most successful and respected cricket nation in the world and to encourage the widest possible participation and interest in the game". The ECB's commitment "to deliver the most effective coach education programme in the world" is therefore pivotal to long term sustainable success.

This will only be achieved if coaching knowledge and the everyday practice of coaches is constantly improving. If this book has achieved its purpose, it will make a contribution to that improvement.

For the established coach, I hope that this book has reinforced many of the practices you already employ, and also introduced you to more ideas to consider. For the coach embarking on a coaching career, I hope it has given you plenty of information to indicate where you might start.

The heart of success will be your preparation, and when that is combined with the integration of the vital ingredients and the crucial factor of communication you will start to make your own luck.

Please remember what was said in the introduction: it's your rucksack; you, and nobody else, decide what to put into it.

BIBLIOGRAPHY

1. The ECB Cricket Coach's Manual
>   This is automatically distributed as a course resource for
>   candidates enrolling on an England and Wales Cricket Board
>   Level I course.

2. Play Better Cricket
>   **by Stephen J. Bull, Scott Fleming & Jo Doust**
>   Published by Sports Dynamics, 1992 ISBN 0 951 9543 0 X

3. The Mental Game Plan – Getting Psyched for Sport
>   **by Stephen J. Bull Ph.D., John G. Albinson Ph. D.,**
>   **and Christopher J. Shambrook Ph. D.**
>   Published by Sports Dynamics, 1996 ISBN 0 951 9543 2 6
>   Reprinted 1997.

References:

1. "The ECB Performance Diary" for Under 15s.
>   One of a series of performance diaries for county under 13, 15, 17
>   and 19-year old age groups. There are sections on performance
>   records, technical, tactical, mental, physical and lifestyle
>   management skills.

2. The Association of Cricket Coaches Journal No. 28 December 1998.
>   Article on "Training for Cricket" by Nigel Stockill.

3. The Association of Cricket Coaches Journal No. 28 December 1998.
>   Article on "Vision Training in Cricket" by Simon Falk and
>   Simon Hollyhead.

4. "The Complete Book of Modern Fielding Practices" by Chris Stone
>   Publishes by Robert Hale, London. 1992 ISBN 0 7090 4857 2

5. "Animated Skill Drills for Cricket Coaching"
>   CD Rom by Tacklesport Consultancy Limited, 1999.

6. "Achievement, Motivation and Attribution Theory" by B. Weiner
>   Published by General Learning Press (Morristown N. J.) 1974 ISBN

7. A motivational speech on "Winning" made by Frank Dick OBE
>   at "Cricket Live 1999" at the Birmingham National Exhibition
>   Centre. This was the ECB's inaugural "World Cricket Coaches
>   Conference and Exhibition".

8. A speech on "Patterns for Success" made by Bob Woolmer
>   at "Cricket Live 1999" at the Birmingham National Exhibition Centre.